What an absolutely beautiful book... Pages of love letters to bread; everything it is, does, and how very special it is as a part of our food vocabulary. Wonderful words by Tim make this book perfect bedtime reading for any foodie but, more importantly, anyone who has ever eaten bread.

Tom Kerridge

●

A book by Tim Hayward is eagerly anticipated. When the subject is his love of bread, its lore and great many uses, his sound, good sense noting the myriad ways in which bread enhances daily life makes this book a most inspiring read. He illuminates each page with his thoughts and love of food in the most endearing of voices.

Jeremy Lee

●

A beautiful love letter to the very first processed food. Any book that contains a section on the joys of crisp sandwiches gets my vote.

Jay Rayner

●

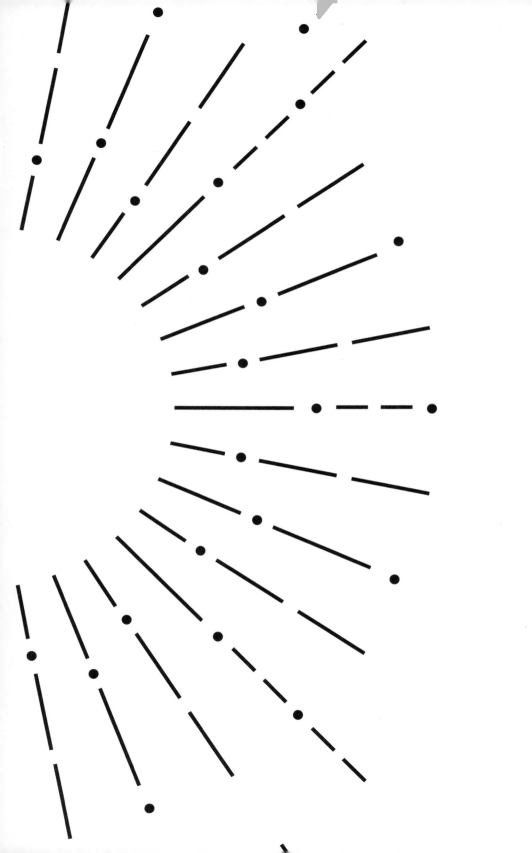

LOAF STORY

*A Love Letter to Bread,
with Recipes*

Tim Hayward

Photography by Sam Folan

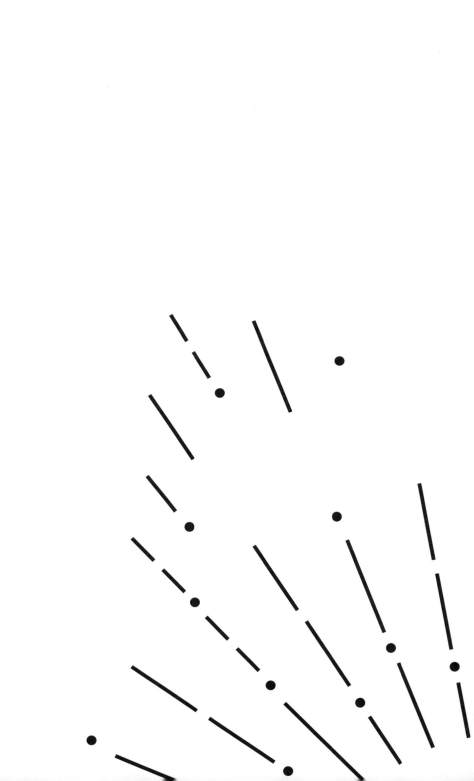

To my mum, Heather, who instilled in me,
amongst many fine and useful things,
her profound love of bread.

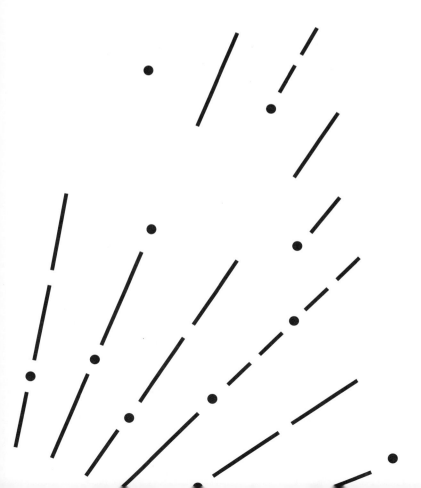

Contents

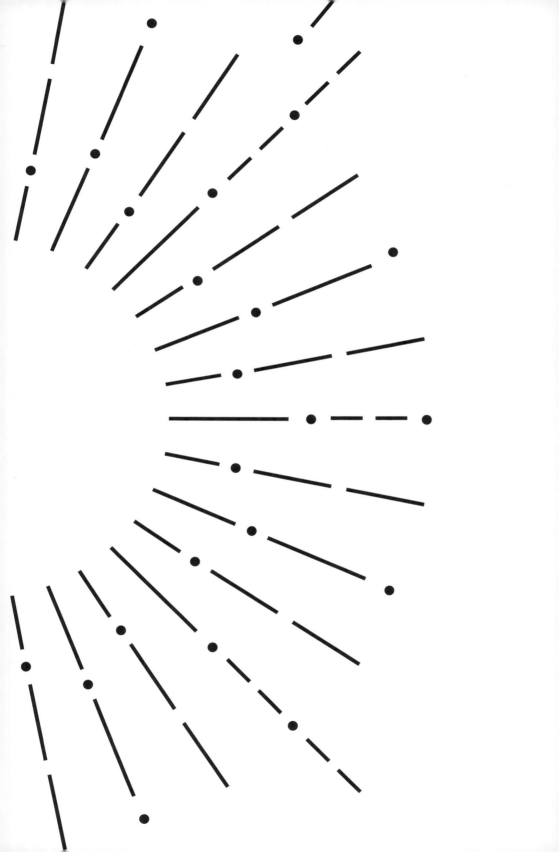

Introduction

There's a single food that I've eaten every day since I was weaned. It's different most days – there are countless ways to make it interesting – but that almost doesn't matter, because, God help me, I love it every way it comes.

Some people think of it as a side dish. They think its presence on a separate little plate alongside the main meal means 'posh'. Others believe eating it with every meal is an infallible indicator of social naffness. Like most things in my country, it's laden with class significance, from its size to its shape.

But in spite of the fact that it's the UK's national staple, it rarely features on menus except as an extra. We still regard it as the defining ingredient of a 'snack' or something informal, grabbed and gobbled. It's been demonised for being mass-produced and for lacking nutritional value at the same time as being so irresistible that it's the root cause of our national obesity crisis. At any given time, you can open a newspaper or magazine and read articles about how this food clogs your insides and adds kilos to your outside. There are popular diets that exclude its consumption entirely, yet it's so powerful a symbol of who we are and aspire to be that *just the smell of it* can, apparently, affect our decision on which house we buy.[1] At times it's been bad, at times it's been good, but never, for a single second, have we fallen out of love with bread.

One of the first meals I can remember, when I was very small and Mum had trouble stretching her budget to feed us, was a slice of supermarket white, fried in carefully saved bacon fat, cut into squares and topped with leftover mash and a blob of ketchup. I have eaten toast in damp flats, caravans, up mountains, in the galleys of boats, in front of roaring fires in impossibly romantic hotels and in thin slices under both foie gras and

---

[1] Empirical evidence that the smell of freshly baked bread can improve your chances of selling your house is, predictably, scant, but what is remarkable is how many presumably intelligent people seem to believe it – how many other foods have an associated culture-wide collective delusion?

dripping. At primary school, small, twitchy and neurotic, I had exactly the same sandwich in my lunchbox for nearly two years. It was a talisman of home that could defend me from the nameless terrors of a horrible institution. They thought I was unadventurous; I knew you didn't mess with the only thing that makes you feel loved. As a teenager, as my mother tells it, I'd come home from school, start toasting a fresh loaf and not stop till it was gone. Later, George Orwell's evocation of the power of 'tea-and-two-slices' as the constant driving fuel of the British working class formed my politics and my food writing.

Bread was the subject of great family tension when I was growing up. My dad was one of three sons in a working-class family, my mum one of the two daughters of a headmaster. For Dad, bread was part of laying the table. A couple of slices of white on the plate, whatever was served, for mopping up any gravy, sauce, juice or other valuable morsel of nourishment. For my grandfather, dad and uncles, eating was a muscular exercise in refuelling with an added layer of competition, and bread was a vital tool and ingredient. If the texture of the meal was right, the sliced bread saw more action than the fork, and if there was ever an occasion when the loaf wasn't there... well, I'm not sure I can recall it.

Mum's family ate bread, too, probably the same brand, but the loaf stayed in the bread bin and never graced the table. You would receive a slice with your dinner if you asked – they were kind and indulgent to portly little grandsons – and there was no stinting on toast or parsimony when Nan 'cut a few rounds of sandwiches', but the loaf stayed in the kitchen.

We are class-obsessed as a nation, but usually not so in personal relationships. My parents, starting a family in the thrillingly democratic 1960s, would never have clashed over money, accent, dress or any of the thousand other signifiers by which the Brits define themselves, but bread was different. For Dad, not having bread on the table was a diminution of the generosity – even the love – demonstrated by his mother. For Mum, it was inappropriate – as much of a dishonour to her new family's table as a lump of coal or an oily spanner.

I should probably reiterate here that this is 'sliced white' we're talking about. Packaged bread, made with the Chorleywood Process (see page 14) and wrapped in gorgeous wax paper (that was later smoothed out, saved and reused for wrapping up school packed lunches). There were two types: medium or thick sliced. There may have been a thin version as well, but I'm sure there's another important class-based reason that I never saw it. Regardless, the key point is that we're discussing the significant differences within a class of bread that today we'd completely reject. There was no 'brown' bread to be had outside of the rare health-food shops, the 'French stick' was an impossibly exotic speciality that nobody quite understood or trusted and a 'crusty' or 'farmhouse' loaf, from a baker, was a treat. Cutting it yourself meant fewer slices per loaf, so it was explicitly, self-evidently, an indulgent luxury.

For a while, Mum bought 'Nimble'. Somebody, somewhere had worked out that bread was 'fattening' and that bread pumped with even more air would be lighter and therefore 'slimming'. There were TV ads showing thin, glamorous young women drifting above wheat fields in hot-air balloons, just to hammer home the notion that this stuff would make you weightless. This was either the high or the low point of British advertising, depending on your point of view, as the main benefit being sold was the voids in the bread created under a vacuum during processing – the most literal case ever of persuading consumers to pay more for absolutely nothing. We all tried it and it was awful… but the idea that bread was somehow both 'bad' in its simplest form, and that it might be offered as a remedy, too, was firmly implanted.

Supermarkets began to stock brown bread, wholemeal and 'granary' entered the family repertoire – not without resistance – and after a while the baguette was revealed to us like a plaster saint to which we could raise our eyes. This was 'proper' bread… and, for a brief flash of time, was devoid of any negative connotation.

From Chorleywood to Bro Bread

A while back I found myself in conversation with a brilliant baker. She's famous in her own country and abroad and has written books on the subject. I admit, drink had been taken and we were comparing notes on the state of baking globally. 'Do you know what?' she said, quite suddenly and with some passion, 'I'm sick of "bro" bread.'

I think I got what she meant the second she said it, but I'd never heard it articulated in that way. Half the world has been baking bread and developing their own ways with it since the very beginnings of civilisation, but for food lovers everywhere, and particularly for a new generation of 'craft bakers', the *sine qua non* is the 'bro loaf'. Coming out of San Francisco, originating perhaps in the sourdough traditions of Europe, it's a big miche with a lacerated dark-baked crust, made from 'interesting' flours and raised with carefully curated, naturally occurring yeasts. It's a truly beautiful thing that, in the imagination at least, would have been at home on any farm table from the Arctic Circle to the southern tip of Spain at any time since the Dark Ages. The problem is that although, compared with mass-produced bread, bro bread is 'full of character', it has no local cultural relevance and, as my friend insisted with increasing frustration, it distracts bakers from the local breads that do.

I've no animus against a brilliant craft sourdough. It's delicious. It also has as much connection to my own food culture as sashimi or an excellent Côtes du Rhône – and God knows, I'd never turn either of those down – but I'm intrigued by the myths we've built around the bro loaf.

It is most often presented as the antithesis to the mass-produced or machine-made loaf, which is to some degree true, and yet, bread is of its very nature an exercise in mass production, no matter how primitive. Except in a few very distant cultures, a single family unit will not grow enough grain to make their own bread. If they do, they are very unlikely to be able to hand grind it successfully enough to make anything beyond porridge. Wheat for flour was one of the first crops we grew collectively. Once an individual in a community managed to get set up for efficient grinding, it was one of the first activities in which labour became specialised. Mills were the first machines to be driven by power sources like wind and water and later by steam.

Fuel has always been expensive, either in terms of money or labour, and it would never have been wasted. For risen loaves, as opposed to flatbreads, you need an oven, which takes a lot of fuel to heat – fuel that is largely wasted in baking a single loaf. Even if loaves were made at home, they would be baked in a community oven, for fuel efficiency. Bread stales within a day, so either the oven ran every day or, as still happens in a few parts of rural Italy, farms formed little collectives where each would bake for the others on one particular day each week. Bread production and the elements of the process that must be undertaken collectively are at the roots of our communities, our nationalities, our cultures and even our politics... but what bread has never been is a solitary art.

It is doubtless good for the soul to form a loaf by hand and to fire your own oven. But if you bake for others, at what point does it become 'commercial'? If you employ a horse-drawn harvester or a windmill, at what point is your bread production 'mechanised'? Did our loaf become 'industrial' the day the town baker could afford an electrically powered dough mixer and an oil-powered oven, no longer working men to an early death through the brutally physical job of doing it by hand?

At a time when we're being told the dangers of 'processed foods', it's worth remembering that bread is the first and most basic of all of them.

There are many bakeries where the work cycle is still based on the size of the 'batch' that the oven can handle, but it is perhaps unsurprising that, when the Industrial Revolution was sparked, the machine-driven mass production of bread (the worker's staple) was the first process to be 'industrialised'.

A white bread loaf that can be shot from a peel onto the hot base of the oven requires skilled hands to make, but dumping a measured lump of dough into a metal mould (a loaf tin) can be done cheaply and quickly by a machine. The shape of our standard national loaf is defined by the industrialisation and deskilling of the baking process.

While the UK was first to standardise the 'tin loaf', France, with full support from the state, developed a national network of small bakeries, which is why, to this day, the defining French loaf is a hand-shaped stick. And while for generations French bakers have concentrated on preserving the traditional art of bakery, their British counterparts have innovated.

Mechanical mixers could be made as big as an engineer could imagine and build, moulding machines could turn out loaves as fast as the dough could be mixed and huge ovens could bake continuously. Baking became faster, cheaper and more efficient, but there was a limiting factor. Rising was the one element of the baking process that remained slow, and the action of live yeast on poorly refined flour was unpredictable. A truly mechanised process of bread manufacture demanded both speed and accurate repeatability. If rising could be properly controlled, there would be no limits on mechanised production.

The earliest attempt to solve the problem of 'proving' came from a Scottish medic, Dr John Dauglish, who founded the Aerated Bread Company in 1862. Like many in his profession at the time, Dauglish saw huge possibilities for the betterment of society through diet and nutrition. He thought that the process of hand kneading[2] was profoundly unhygienic as well as dangerously hard on the bodies of the workers, and that fermentation, involving live bacteria, was a 'destructive influence'. He sought to abolish both processes by aerating the dough with pressurised carbon dioxide – the same process used to put the fizz in sparkling water.

This is not, on the face of it, quite as crazy an idea as it sounds. Yeasts make bread rise by consuming the sugars in the flour and excreting CO_2 into the dough. Mechanical aeration created the same effect without the farting bugs.

Dauglish's company was successful. His patented process spread to the US and Australia. The bread was seen as 'healthy' and clean, the process worked with the increasingly popular wholemeal and Graham flours, and hospitals and institutions bought it in large quantities. Though his motives in creating the process seem to have been entirely altruistic, his method meant bread could be made faster, in more mechanised processes and thus more cheaply, and so it drove many more traditional bakers to the wall. Eventually the company opened a popular chain of tearooms.

Mention Chorleywood to most serious bread bakers and you'll see a flash of anger cross their faces. It's one of those 'don't mention the war' subjects, and it was, in many ways, a battle that bread lovers lost. Chorleywood was a bucolic little village in Hertfordshire with few claims to distinction save the presence of the British Baking Industries Research Association. It was at their research station that, in 1961, the Chorleywood Bread Process was born and bread changed forever for at least half the consumers in the world.

[2] He also mentions kneading with the feet, an idea that, if true, must have thoroughly appalled consumers.

For many years the UK had imported 'strong' wheat with a high protein content from other parts of the world. Strong flour, loaded with gluten, makes an elastic dough that allows lots of strong bubbles to form as the bread rises. Stronger bubbles mean a lighter crumb and greater volume – in short, a better loaf. Dauglish's aeration process required very strong flour. British wheat, though, tended to be 'soft' – i.e. containing less gluten protein. Local flour made great cakes and pastries, good buns and lovely pie crusts, but the expanding market for high-quality white bread made the UK dependent on the prairies of Canada, the American Midwest and even Russia.

The Chorleywood Process made light, airy bread from softer, cheaper, local flour by 'mechanical development'. First, fat, vitamin C and yeast are added to the dough, and then it is beaten forcibly by high-powered processors that incorporate CO_2 (or other gases) into the dough. The dough is stored, for short periods of time, in sealed vessels in which the air pressure in the headspace can be controlled. When the pressure is lowered, the bubbles in the dough expand, meaning that the operator can effectively 'dial in' the airiness of the dough and it is no longer dependent on the yeast for anything more than taste.

There is no reason that Chorleywood bread can't be delicious – 80 per cent of the bread consumed in the UK is made this way with few complaints – but it also gave manufacturers a lot of tools that could be horribly misused. An early development of the process was a clutch of highly aerated 'slimmers' breads', including the Nimble my mum tried. Industrial bakers were also able to pander to the lowest tastes of mass consumers. Given the choice, consumers wanted whiter bread – with fewer nutrients. They favoured softer crusts that were easier to eat and a moister, sweeter crumb. They demanded a longer shelf life, which meant the addition of fats and moisture-trapping additives, and the longer life, often in plastic wrapping, meant preservatives were necessary to prevent mould.

During two world wars, with bread production a strategic imperative, government had supported and relied on the biggest industrial bakeries. In peacetime these huge companies were able to write their own rules. The bakeries managed to lobby for a partial exemption from labelling laws so that 'flour enhancers' did not have to be specified by individual name or quantity. By the end of the twentieth century, mass-produced bread in

Britain was in a pretty scandalous state. A standard family 'white sliced' had evolved into a block of barely cooked, mechanically aerated dough, with a sweet, soft crust and embalmed with a truckload of additives. It was 'easy to eat' and in many ways enjoyable, but was it even bread any more?

It's argued, convincingly, by craft bakers that much of our almost epidemic 'intolerance' to bread products is as attributable to unseen additives and mechanised production as it is to gluten.

This all makes it sound like a sliced white loaf might be the most appalling thing you could put in your body, and yet it has some amazing qualities. It was the most popular bread over a couple of centuries when some of the best sandwiches came into being. Its consistency, blandness and sweetness, its shape and its structural integrity made it a vital, irreplaceable element of some of the most genuinely iconic sandwich recipes.

For all its shonkiness, its flavour and texture are unique – perhaps not 'real bread', yet something without parallel that cannot help but tap deep into our sense memories – pappy, plasticky and preservative-laden, but perfectly Proustian.[3]

Really, though, the point at which your bro bread can lose its claim to be artisanal is all a matter of degree. God knows, I've no desire to blow up the whole trend and return to extruded Chorleywood pap, whatever its status as a symbol of our past, but perhaps it's time to pause. Vanishingly few of our food traditions are pre-industrial, and most of our best come from a time when agriculture and food production were mechanised and the majority of the population were urban dwellers, distanced from food production. We have grown up loving non-bro bread. For me, to deny that is not just foolishly romantic… it's dangerously false.

---

[3] My own most Proustian memory of sliced white comes from travelling on Southern Region trains from Bournemouth to London as a starving art student. The only thing I could afford in the dining car was toast. Two pieces of medium-sliced white Mother's Pride, toasted in a gas salamander and then dressed with hot, salty Anchor butter, kept liquid in a can above the range and applied with a four-inch paintbrush.

A few years ago I bought a bakery and now my life is filled with bread. I didn't plan it that way, but looking back, it seems weirdly inevitable. So now I want to write about bread. Not making it – others do that far better than me – but appreciating all the ways we enjoy it. And not just posh bread or artisanal bread, but all the different loaves we eat every day of our lives. I want to explore the quirks and lore of our daily bread and share the strange recipes I've collected and loved.

In a way it's a Life Story. It's certainly a Love Letter. In fact, it's a Loaf Story.

A Note About Recipes

I freely admit that I'm not a recipe person. I read them, with almost indecent avidity. I'm looking right now at about twenty running metres of bookshelf laden with thousands of the damned things, but when I go into the kitchen I don't take them with me. I suppose part of the pleasure of reading them, for me, is trying to understand the principles *behind* the measurements and instructions so that when I stand in the kitchen slinging food about, it's a natural process. I know. It's incredibly irritating and immature. I suppose the main thing, though, is that once I get started, I cook on a wave of enthusiasm… chopping, tasting, seasoning… sometimes it feels like seat-of-the-pants stuff, like driving a fast car or how a musician must feel when improvising. Oh God, I should probably be beaten up for the metaphor but, it's a bit like *jazz*. I've obsessively studied the standards, I understand the structure and bones of what I'm doing and where I want to be and, yes, at least half the time the result is self-indulgent, noodling crap. But sometimes it might just make fellow nerds nod their heads in appreciation.

When we started planning how this book would look, I finally had to admit that I just don't have the literary chops to sustain joy and enthusiasm at the same time as trying to capture every single weight, measure, time and technique in a way that can be clearly conveyed, so my genius of a publisher suggested I split it. In the body of the text I've been encouraged to write how I cook, then, with infinite care, we've written terse, concise and forensically accurate kitchen instructions in a separate section. For me, this is an entirely liberating change… I hope I can communicate it to you.

On
Bread

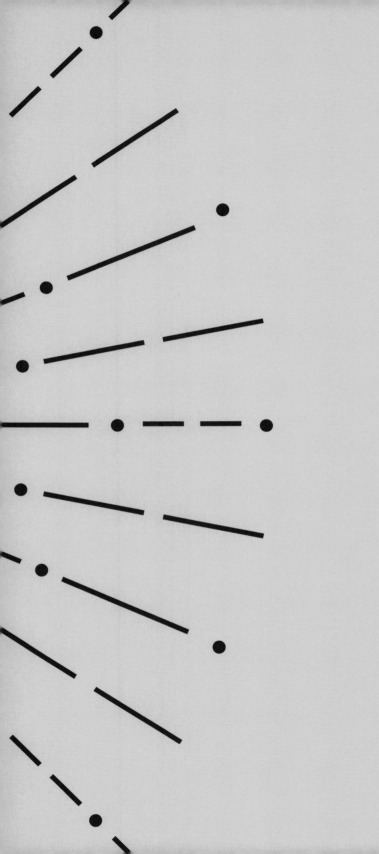

First Principle – Toast

It is impossible to undertake any serious consideration of bread without first discussing toast. Yes, bread is gorgeous, but it's usually cold, it can be a bit floppy and insubstantial and it tends to go stale quickly. Toasting is the answer to all these issues… and then oh so much more. Toast is a world of its own; the substrate for astonishing cuisine across the globe, and in the UK a near obsession for a whole nation.

Do you and your partner like your toast the same way? If you do, you are not only creepily compatible but a statistically insignificant anomaly. Even when you take two adjacent slices from the same loaf – an effective metaphor for total similarity – there are so many variations in *cuisson*, serving temperature, butter application strategies and quantities… and that's before you even take the lid off the jam/marmalade/Marmite.

If you ever needed a convenient symbol for the British oddness around toast, consider for a moment the toast rack and all that it represents. It should be self-evident that toast is best hot from the grill, fire or toaster so that the butter can melt and the full fortifying effects of the heat can be appreciated. It would be daft, surely, to *plan* for toast to go cold – and yet that is exactly what many toast aficionados do. Place a slice of hot toast on a plate and it will go cold. On the upper surface, steam will rise, but on the underside, it will be trapped and the moisture reabsorbed into the slice. It will become soggy.

Sadly, I have come to realise that there are people who actively like soggy, cold toast, but they are mercifully few and they usually keep their vice a secret. The toast rack is designed to let the toast go cold while staying crisp. Now, this could just be another insane variable in the wild palette of toast preferences, but there are, as so often happens in the UK, class distinctions at work here.

Anyone who makes toast in a domestic setting can arrange for it to be served hot and delicious. From a toasting fork, off the top of the Aga, from an eye-level grill or just out of a regular toaster, most of us can literally turn upon a heel and have the real deal dropped onto the plate from scorched fingers. The first electric toasters were attractive little items designed to sit in the middle of the breakfast table or, judging from gushing newspaper ads, on a tray while sitting up in bed. Hot toast is easy to acquire everywhere except the most aristocratic households, grand hotels, officers' messes or boarding-school dining rooms, for it is here that the toast is made in bulk in the kitchen and carried by staff to the table. A taste for cold, crisp toast is an infallible indicator, apparently, of the right sort of upbringing, or of an aspiration to it. Like the cruet and the fish knife, the toast rack sits forever in the armoury of those who 'must have things daintily served'.

Having dealt with the cooling of toast, we should pause for a moment to consider 'doneness', colour or, more accurately, the degree of burning. It's the browned stuff that carries the toast flavour. Victorian cookery books are full of innovative suggestions to utilise this. There are recipes for 'toast water', in which the cooked, crisp surface of the toast is grated with a purpose-made 'rasp' into clear water for feeding to invalids.[4] A more luxe variation would be any of the dozens of recipes, from all over the world, for 'milk toast', in which the toast is soaked in milk, lending it flavour and softening any troubling crustiness. Mrs Beeton herself recommends a 'toast sandwich', in which a well-toasted slice is placed between two thickly buttered slices of 'raw' bread.[5] Actually, it's pretty good.

For reasons nobody can quite remember, it was once considered rather refined to toast two slices of bread sandwiched together. That would provide the benefit of one crisp and browned side and one hot, steamed one. À chacun son goût. Perhaps it was something about saving fuel or speeding up production. Or perhaps it was an intentional reversal of the method for making 'Melba toasts', which for decades were the first thing taught to kids learning 'domestic science' in school. For these, a slice is toasted (both sides), allowed to cool in a rack and then carefully sliced through the middle, creating two even thinner slices that are then toasted on their raw side to produce something that's laden with 'toasted' flavour and shatters in the mouth like an expensive biscuit.

[4] I have tried really hard to understand how this could make anyone feel better. I've made it a couple of times and it made me feel measurably worse.
[5] *Mrs Beeton's Book of Household Management* (1861).

It's hard to think of anything more benign than the innocent pursuit of toasty flavour and yet, in recent decades, a new fear has grown around 'burntness' in food. One of the products of charring (burning something to blackness) is acrylamide, very high doses of which have been shown to increase the risk of cancer in laboratory mice. The IARC (International Agency for Research on Cancer) considers it 'probably carcinogenic to humans'.[6] For a decade or so, the notion has grown that 'burnt' toast is 'bad' and will kill us all. It's certainly hampered the enjoyment of those who favour the darker tones in the palette of toast.

In 2017 the UK Food Standards Agency launched a 'Go for Gold' campaign to encourage the British public to cook food – particularly starches – only to the point of golden brownness, to minimise the production of acrylamide. This would have appalled my grandfather who liked his toast properly incinerated so that he 'could taste it'. It also ran counter to the findings of a 2015 study undertaken by the European Food Safety Authority that 'acrylamide intake was not associated with an increased risk of most common cancers, including those of the GI or respiratory tract, breast, prostate and bladder'.[7] Today, Cancer Research UK states on its website that 'for most cancer types, there is no link between acrylamide and cancer risk'.[8] Once again, it seems that, as government gets its act together to demonise something officially, actual scientific thought is shifting towards the position that it's fine in moderation… unless you're a mouse being force-fed burnt toast.

The toaster is probably the most ubiquitous single-use device in most western domestic kitchens. You might have a deep-fat fryer for frying things or a mixer for mixing them… but a single machine just to scorch the surface of single slices of bread? That's remarkably specific.

The glory days of toast really began with urbanisation. When large numbers of people moved into restricted accommodation, with inadequate cooking facilities, toast came into its own. In a house with no kitchen it's difficult to get a hot meal on the table, but in a room with a fire, a loaf of bread and a tin of sardines something gorgeous begins to happen.

[6] …as are many chemicals, red meat, shift-work and a career in hairdressing.
[7] https://efsa.onlinelibrary.wiley.com/doi/epdf/10.2903/j.efsa.2015.4104
[8] https://www.cancerresearchuk.org/about-cancer/causes-of-cancer/diet-and-cancer/food-controversies#food_controversies0

On Toast

The principal joy in eating hot toast is the application of much butter. This is certainly what most Brits will tell you, but it conceals a more fundamental and global truth. We eat our toast with *salted* butter and so fail to make the connection that every other bread-eating culture does with bread and salt. Bread and salt are offered in ritual greeting across most Nordic and Slavic countries, right across Central Europe and in the Middle East. Welcome your guest by offering bread, but including salt, too, implies more – the wish that he will eat it; that he will break the bread with you. It is true that we tend to salt our bread in the baking more than others might, but really we get the salt kick we need from the butter we use.

Butter is made by churning the fat out of milk and draining the liquid portion away. In most other butter-eating nations – those that don't rely on olive oil or pork fat as their lubricating grease of choice – the butter is then allowed to ferment for a while to aid preservation. Historically, we don't ferment our butter much at all. Perhaps in our cooler climate it wasn't thought necessary or perhaps we just ate it so damn fast we didn't need to store it for months and just churned up fresh batches, but mainly we preserved our butter by salting. As it's the fermentation that turns butter from white to yellow, we also had to add a colourant, and, in some cases, churn extra cream back into the butter to render it blander and richer. The Brits are unique in rejecting butter that's too pronouncedly 'buttery' as rancid, preferring it blandly flavoured and really quite heavily salted.

Today, of course, manufacturers are reducing salt in every product wherever they possibly can and as a result we're sold more unsalted and 'lightly salted' butter in supermarkets – but those of us with longer gustatory memories can never forget the commercial butter of our childhood: alarmingly yellow and astringently salty. It is perhaps unsurprising that for most of us, our recollections of the first 'foreign' breads we encountered were 'unsalted' and with pale and unsalted butter. A French baguette has little salt in it and an Italian or Spanish loaf will have none at all. In Tomás Graves' amazing book *Bread & Oil* (2000) he lays out a comprehensive list of the different ways with bread on the Balearic Islands: with fruity olive oil, raw garlic or overripe and juicy tomatoes in a *pa amb tomàquet*, but always with the addition of salt… it's so obvious that it's part of the picture and yet it's somehow so intrinsic to the consumption of bread that it doesn't even warrant mentioning in the title.

But perhaps we Brits have pushed things a little further in our pursuit of saltiness. How else can we explain the truly odd things that only we spread on our toast?

Marmite was invented by Baron Justus von Liebig towards the end of the nineteenth century.[9] To be strictly accurate, he was responsible for the discovery that yeast could be concentrated into a highly nutritious paste, which, as with many of his discoveries, he believed could be used to feed the poor and malnourished. The founders of the Marmite company, realising that yeast was available by the tonne as a waste product of the brewing industry, set up a factory in Burton-on-Trent, in the West Midlands of England. Liebig had been excited by the idea that yeast extract was a potent source of vitamins B1, 2, 3 and 9,[10] but that's not what drove customers to consume it like addicts. Marmite contains lots of free glutamic acids – basically natural monosodium glutamate (MSG) – and the yeast is extracted by autolysis, breaking down the yeast cells with huge amounts of salt. Yes, Marmite is basically yummy salt and tasty MSG in a conveniently gluey spread, capable of adhering to bread and enhancing it.[11] If – and God knows I'd love to – we were to set up something like the US space programme, wherein billions of dollars and the best scientific minds of the world were employed in the search for the single, perfect material for the English to spread on toast, the result, after decades of experiment and extraordinary expenditure, would be Marmite.

[9] A phenomenal chemist, Liebig was responsible for a long list of developments in the manufacturing of food for a burgeoning urban working class. He discovered the use of ammonia as a nitrogenous fertiliser, invented the first safe infant formula and, through his Liebig's Extract of Meat Company based in Fray Bentos, Uruguay (yes, it is really a place), brought us corned beef, Bovril and, indirectly, Oxo. There should be a statue in Trafalgar Square to this German genius, who did so much for the way we eat in the UK.
[10] Vitamin B12 isn't naturally found in yeast extract and so is added.
[11] Much as I'm sure a scientist of Liebig's stature would have been fascinated by MSG and the 'umami' effect it produces, it wasn't isolated as a food product until 1908.

They say that everyone either loves Marmite or hates it, but it isn't half as polarising as Gentleman's Relish, which many people will not admit into their house. Gentleman's Relish was formulated by an Englishman called John Osborn, who launched it at one of the large 'expositions' in Paris in (depending on your source) either 1828, 1849 or 1855. I like to think he might have tried all three in a determined attempt to get the world's most food-obsessed nation to understand something so utterly weird. Also known as Patum Peperium (cod Latin for 'spiced paste'), Gentleman's Relish is a highly spiced anchovy butter, which, like Marmite, is tongue-shrivellingly salty. One is instructed to smear this stuff on toast in an incredibly thin layer and perhaps to mitigate it with lots of emollient scrambled eggs to make the classic 'savoury', Scotch woodcock.

There is no doubt that all the very best things on toast or bread bring some degree of saltiness to the party, often combined with delicious, buttery fat and some element of umami. I find the modern execution of Gentleman's Relish too muddy-flavoured and, frankly, weak for my taste, so I prefer to make my own anchovy butter.

It's a simple process that would have delighted Liebig in its use of a fortunate by-product. I love expensive tinned or jarred anchovies in oil, but nobody else in my family cares for them. Actually, it's worse than that; everyone else leaves the room when I open a jar. I find three anchovies, dressed in their own oil, on a slice of fresh white sourdough with a few additional crumbs of salt and perhaps a couple of drops of sherry vinegar a superlative snack, but I'm then left with the rest of the jar to deal with. I chill the remaining anchovies in their oil until it solidifies, then weigh the resulting mixture. I add twice the amount of fridge-cold butter, a little Espelette pepper and the merest scraping of lemon zest and then blitz the lot in a small spice blender. The resulting anchovy butter gets rolled in a piece of greaseproof paper and frozen – leaving no problematic, smelly leftovers in the fridge, but providing me with a sort of fragrant candle of solid butter from which I can crack a chunk in the morning and allow it to melt over my hot toast.

Perhaps I'm no gentleman but I find no need to spread this stuff thinly or to weaken it with eggs. The only special treatment it needs is extra bread for a second slice.

Beans on Toast

To start with the very first principles of this culinary medium, we should turn our attention to beans on toast. It constitutes probably the simplest proper meal you can eat with a plate and cutlery but can be prepared with next to no equipment. As long as you can stick a bit of bread in the toaster and find some way of taking the chill off the beans, you're a bedsit Escoffier.[12]

Baked beans can, of course, be quite a performance. God knows I have spent many hours pursuing the perfect homemade Boston baked beans. I've salted my own pork, lined the base of an ancient earthenware crock with pig skin, packed it with soaked beans and poured on mustard, molasses and a dozen secret aromats. I've sealed it closed and buried the whole kit in a hole in the ground heated with live coals and waited twenty-four hours. They were good. After that much effort I'd have been bloody livid if they weren't.

I've 'baked' beans in pressure cookers, in *sous vide* baths and crock pots and they've all been delicious, but the terrible truth is that none of them were tinned Heinz baked beans. I know, you're expecting the standard disclaimer that 'other brands of sauced bean are available', but c'mon. We know the truth. Heinz beans are *sui generis*, entirely and utterly a thing on their own. They have the same relationship to any homemade beans that tinned peaches do to fresh ones. They are the same at a genetic level, but as different as you can possibly imagine in real life.

Even the greatest, most complex and highly wrought works of art must begin with sketches. Loose first principles. The blocks that may or may not form the bones of the eventual work. These foundations must be simple, fashioned from the most basic of media, with the possibilities of

---

[12] Hardcore purists can even do without the toast and a pan for the beans. I recently interviewed some young soldiers about ration packs and they said they preferred beans in plastic pouches because they could heat them up by tucking them inside their body armour, for a fortifying warm snack when they returned from patrol.

embellishment severely pared back. Baked beans are the starting point, the base camp for any ascent of the mountain of toast. Books could be written on the various creative enhancements, but mastery of basic beans on toast is an essential first step.

Think first of the bread. It should be uncontroversial to rule out all but white bread. Nutty flavours, complexity and pronounced textures would all run counter to the basic traits of the beans' sweet, douce, naïve flavours, unchallenging in the mouth. Packaged white bread would be perhaps too sweet unless balanced by salty bacon or sausages elsewhere on the plate. Yes, save the Mother's Pride to be fried and nestled under eggs and beans in your full fry-up. Baked beans will be shown to their best advantage on a slice of toasted sourdough where the sourness can play against the sweetness of the beans like a squirt of lemon juice in a cocktail.

You could just mound your hot beans on the bread, and you'd have done a grand thing. You'd have primed a perfect canvas and, as a mere apprentice in Leonardo's studio, that would have gained you praise and plaudits. But, as ever, even in a work of bold simplicity, it is the tiny refinements that will mark you out as a master in your own right.

We can kid ourselves – and many do – that beans on toast is a modest, restrained dish, almost the opposite of luxurious; and yet, take a discreet gander at those people's use of butter and you'll see through the delusion. 'Ample' butter is probably not quite enough. You need it hot, salty, melted and combining with the sauce of the beans in a golden slick, running over the crust and imperilling your shirt front as you raise the fork to your lips.

They say that one of the symptoms of aging is a coarsening of the palate, particularly in relation to salt, to which the old are considered to have become desensitised to a ridiculous degree. Naturally, I don't buy this idea with anywhere near as much enthusiasm as the widespread conspiracy theory that 'they're cutting down the salt'. Whatever the truth, I find even Heinz are a bit bland these days, which gives us the opportunity to whip in either some Worcestershire sauce or sriracha (never both). Both are laden with glutamates, so they replace the missing salt with an even more powerful flavour enhancer.

Sardines on Toast

The smell and texture of sardines has, sadly, fallen out of favour. Perhaps there are too many other easily available and less-challenging flavours; perhaps we can't get past the taint of poverty that sardines still seem to represent, but we're missing a trick here. Sardines tick so many boxes of modern eating – healthy, sustainable and a source of pretty much pure umami – that it's worth our making a serious effort to relearn how good they are.[13] Sardines are packed with vitamins, minerals and only the healthiest of fats, but contain no carbohydrates. While a few health enthusiasts might think that is a great thing, the rest of us, for centuries now, have realised that nothing goes better with sardines than an underlying layer of toast.

I think it's possible to choose your genre for sardines on toast depending on which part of the dish's cultural heritage you want to evoke. You could choose an unsalted rustic loaf in the Spanish style, toast the bread over an open flame and rub it with garlic and oil it before laying out the fish in

[13] The sardine isn't a species of fish. It's the name given to a variety of small fish from the Clupeidae family, usually when referred to as food. What constitutes a sardine varies depending on where you are in the world, but in the FAO/WHO Codex Alimentarius the entry for 'canned sardines' lists twenty-one species that can be used, while the UK Sea Fish Industry Authority unhelpfully defines sardines as immature pilchards – unhelpful because the rest of the world seems to think sardines and pilchards are interchangeable terms for the same thing.

There are a few reasons why clupeids have become humanity's most important food fish. Firstly, they are absurdly plentiful at certain times. They form enormous shoals, sometimes quite close to shore, and can be netted easily in abundance. They are easy to process. A skilled gutter can get the guts and sometimes the bones out of a sardine with the push of a well-aimed thumb, and, if they're really good, can have the head off at the same time. As the sardine has skin rather than scales, the fish can come off the boat and be ready to cook in seconds.

Clupeidae are oily fish, giving them a high nutritive value but also a tendency to go rancid quickly. Preserving the fish in bulk, though, is easy. Like anchovies, they can be packed tightly into barrels with salt and they rapidly cure to a delicious product that will keep for years. Before the advent of refrigerated transportation, this meant that the fish could then be shipped inland in their tubs, forming one of the [*cont...*]

ON BREAD

an oleaginous phalanx. Or you could choose a baguette, toast it over a gas flame, mash the sardines and oil into the surface and top with a couple of rings of onion as a relish. Drink a barbarous Provençal rosé with it and imagine yourself on the dockside in Marseille. Personally I think sardines should tap into my own, more dour culture. I imagine them being eaten in a bedsit in a Patrick Hamilton novel… somewhere in Earl's Court or Brighton, a greasy pea-souper fog pawing insistently at the cracked sash… a shilling in the gas meter to dry the last pair of nylons and to toast the thick-cut white bloomer from the corner shop… a little hoarded butter… I think I'd need the ferocious yellow colouring and extra salt of some old-brand supermarket stuff, and the cold sardines forked onto the seared surface of the hot toast while the butter was still sinking into it.

I find it strange and a little sad that the most fashionable restaurants in London will now bring you a slice of their house-made sourdough and an actual tin of staggeringly expensive anchovies from Spain or Portugal and consider they've served you the most refined of appetisers. I shall not really rest easy until they bring me a tin of sardines, a gas fire and a toasting fork. A couple of rounds of that and I could work up enough angst to write *Hangover Square*.

13 *(cont.)* most popular cheap proteins for the growing urban working class and for armies, navies, travellers and prisoners.

With industrialisation, canning took over from salting and curing as an even more efficient mode of preservation. The gutted fish could be smoked, steamed or fried before packing or even sealed into the metal container with oil or a sauce and cooked inside the tin. Old cans of sardines sometimes turn up in shipwrecks or deserted arctic outposts and, if the seal is still good, they can be eaten by a courageous culinary enthusiast without ill effect. Small Clupeidae shoal all over the world, so canneries sprang up from Iceland and the Falklands, Cornwall and California, to India, Portugal, Norway and Peru.

The conventional can for sardines has always been a single-serving size that can be opened with a ring pull or an attached key. In most countries, the can is 100 per cent recyclable… which probably makes the canned sardine one of the best-ever forms of portable human food, then and now.

Devilled Kidneys

Devilled kidneys, it could be argued, are one of the most highly evolved toppings for toasted bread. Where a rarebit sits on top and *pa amb tomàquet* grinds tomato and garlic into the bread (see page 48), devilled kidneys are made with a large quantity of good gravy that's designed to entirely soak the toast. Once served and cool enough to eat, the tender offal is texturally barely distinguishable from the softened, moist, meaty substrate. The closest thing to it I can think of is the way that stale sponge, once soaked, is entirely integral to a trifle.

But first, let's step back a bit here and look at the 'sop'. It's a word you never hear in a culinary context any more, probably because of its rather unappetising connotations, but historically, something cheap that could 'sop up' flavourful liquids and transform them into a nourishing, fulfilling solid was a useful ingredient to a cook.

Sops crop up in the Bible, Homer and Virgil, where bread is soaked variously in water, wine or broth. The words 'sop' and 'soup' come from the same Germanic root, so there's something very deep in their symbiosis. In medieval England it was common to float a piece of spiced toast in hot wine to create a sort of damp tapa and it's possible that the word 'toast', meaning a blessing or compliment paid over a raised glass, refers back to this practice.

Later, as small game recipes became popular at aristocratic tables, there developed a practice of serving birds on a piece of toast that would soak up any leaking juices. Once hunting with a gun became possible, small game birds worked particularly well on toast. Snipe and woodcock are miracles of natural engineering. Their muscle-to-weight ratio is finely tuned so that they can fly fast enough and with enough agility to avoid predators. To keep up this evasive action they have evolved a way to lighten themselves at takeoff by ejecting all unnecessary weight – namely, all waste matter and superfluous liquid. When taking to the air, not to put too fine a point on it, they defecate completely and explosively.

Be serious for a minute. This means that, if you can knock a bird out of the air as it takes off, it has already voided itself of anything unpleasant

to eat. Get rid of the beak and feathers and you're oven-ready. This is precisely how snipe and woodcock are cooked at their best, with the guts intact. And this is also where the toast comes in. The swiftly roasted bird, flavoured with the entrails, can be eaten easily with knife and fork, but the guts themselves are best hoicked out, mashed and spread on toast to make them more manageable.

All this is a roundabout way of explaining why the idea of rich meat on soaked toast was not immediately objectionable to the aristocratic palate and how, seamlessly, devilled kidneys on toast became a favourite country-house breakfast and gentlemen's club savoury.

It's now common knowledge amongst cooks that cheap cuts are the most flavourful and that offal is often the very best of the cheap stuff. In the days before refrigeration, meat could be hung and stored so that it had a high sale value, but offal would putrefy fast. It rarely left the farm and therefore had a reputation as a low-class junk meat, suitable only for the poor and desperate. In the particular case of kidneys, their reputation was further clouded by their smell. Kidneys that haven't been scrupulously cleaned at slaughter smell of urine. The texture and flavour of their meat, though, is little short of sublime. Like liver, kidneys have no fibrous muscularity, but they lack that iron-y tang and gritty texture that the blood-packed liver suffers from. Having come from inside the body of the animal, a fresh kidney, freed from the core – which is the only part of the organ in physical contact with the urine – is clean to the point of near sterility. Good kidneys can be eaten so lightly cooked that they're effectively raw in the centre.

For Edwardian authenticity you could devil your kidneys in a chafing dish over a spirit lamp, but you'll do perfectly well in a regular frying pan on a normal stove. I'd reckon on three small lambs' kidneys per person for a main course.

Core the kidneys (see page 36), halve them if you wish, then toss them in flour that has been generously seasoned with English mustard powder, and cayenne pepper. Heat some clarified butter[14] in a frying pan until it

[14] Clarified butter gets hotter without burning, while retaining its lovely butteriness. Just melt a pat in a small pan, leave it to separate, then put it in the fridge. The clarified butter will solidify, so you can prise it out of the container, pour away the milky, creamy nonsense and rinse it with cold water.

starts to bubble, then drop in the floured kidneys and toss them about vigorously so that the butter soaks the flour on all sides and starts to form a crisp crust. Don't worry if bits of the crust flake off into the pan; they just add to the general gaiety of nations when we get to the wet ingredients.

Cooking time depends very much on the size of your kidneys, the heat of your pan and how much you keep everything moving, but generally speaking I find that rareness is an advantage and that you're going to want to cook this again and again, so you'll have a chance to refine your own timings. I would rarely take the searing stage longer than a minute, though.

Now it's time to hit the booze. A couple of tablespoons or so of sweetish sherry would not be wrong in the circumstances, or a similar quantity of port. If you want to cut back on any sweetness and/or you require the validation and reassurance of a plume of flame, you could use brandy and set light to it at the appropriate point. Cook off most of the alcohol and you'll have a treacly liquid in the bottom of the pan, partially thickened by the seasoned dredging flour, sizzling aggressively. Before it dries out and starts to catch, add a really substantial amount of Worcestershire sauce or Henderson's relish and then, before that gets a chance to reduce, about half a wine glass of strong stock – beef or chicken will do.

Now for the bread. Flavour here is not the issue – the sauce will supply everything – but the texture is crucial. You'll need white bread in a thick enough slice that a chunk cut out of it will hold on your fork and not fall apart even when sopping with juices. Two centimetres (almost an inch) is not an unreasonable thickness. Devilled kidneys come out of the pan only marginally less hot than the molten core of Mercury, so you will need to let things sit and soak for a while before you dare risk a mouthful. A strong crust will yield in this time and yet provide an interesting textural variation. What you don't want is holes. An artisanal sourdough is a lovely thing, but if the baker's having an off morning and there are big bubbles through the loaf, you're going to end up with a lot of gravy on your shirt and that's a terrible thing to have to explain to your valet. Given the choice, I'd go for a white, bloomer-shaped loaf from the bakery in a good supermarket, perhaps one that's been allowed a day or two to stale. If your bread is very fresh you can briefly introduce it to the toaster, but not for long enough to really colour it. You don't want to cut down the absorbency by any degree at all. However you choose to prepare it, you'll need one slice per serving and a second for 'contingencies'.

Coring Kidneys

Going in through one side of the kidney you'll see a tough, white tube, usually called the core. This branches out inside the organ and is the pipework through which the urine is excreted. Some chefs and a few butchers like to remove the core by grasping it firmly in the fingers, working their way down the 'trunk' with a knife and then carefully cutting each 'branch', leaving the whole kidney intact. Many recipes suggest you halve the kidneys anyway, so it's also fine to split them and then remove the core more easily this way. I used to struggle with this until I found myself cooking one day with a friend who's a medic. Two weeks later he'd furnished me with a haemostat, a pair of Littauer suture scissors and a brief crash course in blunt dissection and renal physiology.

To swiftly remove the kidney's core, clamp the haemostat onto the thickest part of the core and pull upwards. Looking inside the kidney you'll see where the first branches are pulling up, so you can slide in the tip of the scissors and snip through. The partially freed core will then pull further, revealing another set of branches. After a couple more snips and tugs you'll have one last branch to go through before the whole thing is out and you can bask in the applause of the entire surgical team.

Lift out your kidneys onto a plate and allow them to rest for a moment. If they release any juices, pour them straight back into the pan. Continue reducing the sauce until it's a thick gravy consistency… no, I know that's less than useless as an instruction. The point is, how do *you* like *your* gravy? Take it to the consistency you prefer – you can always let it down a little with stock if it gets too thick – then spoon enough onto the bread to cover it convincingly (probably about half of it). Now arrange the kidneys on top of the gravy and pour the rest over the kidneys, the bread and the plate. Serve immediately.

It's unusual to give instructions for eating – it may even be patronising – but kidneys are one of those special tastes that tend to appeal to cooks and food enthusiasts and vaguely nauseate their loved ones, so I'm confident I'm speaking to both chef and diner here; that you've probably done this as a treat for yourself. If all your judgements have been correct, you'll be able to make each forkful a perfect mix of kidney and soaked bread, and if your timing is absolutely precise, you'll end up with a gleaming clean plate, having mopped every last sumptuous atom of the gravy into the bread as you've eaten. If you're less efficient, or perhaps still in a training phase, you might end up with some gravy on the plate. While we must always strive for perfection, luckily you've got the Contingency Slice waiting to polish off any last vestiges of glorious sauce.

Shellfish on Toast

Once you've accepted precisely how well a lightly toasted, grilled or fried slice of bread works as an elegant presentational device, a sop for juices or a replacement for the starch in a more traditional dish, a world of opportunity presents itself. Pretty much any dish you can remember where you've wanted to mop up the juices with a bit of bread at the end becomes a suitable topping. Think about mushrooms in a cream sauce, or some sort of Mediterranean fishy stew. The world is your oyster… or indeed any bivalve mollusc.

You know how good the juices of *moules marinière* are, and how fantastic the flavoursome oil coating the linguine in a *vongole* is… it's just a matter of tweaking them a bit to stay on top of some bread. If you can't get your hands on fresh mussels or clams, the freezer aisle in your local supermarket will probably reveal vacuum-packed options.

Put some finely minced shallots and a crushed clove of garlic in the bottom of a sauté pan or saucepan for which you have a lid. Pour in a

sizeable glug of white wine or, better still, vermouth. Not too much – you want a fragrant steam, not a Jacuzzi. Bring it up to a light simmer, then pour in your shellfish (along with any juices in the pouch if they're the frozen kind). Put the lid on and shake the pan energetically. After about thirty seconds take a peek inside. Some of the shells should be opening. Keep shaking and checking until most of the shells are open, then take the pan off the heat and remove the lid.

I must make it absolutely clear here that I cannot, in all conscience, even consider the idea of tweezers in my kitchen. Their use as a chef tool seems to sum up everything I abhor about pretentious cooking… and yet I find myself forced to permit them for one task and one task only. Until I am allowed to keep a very small monkey with asbestos gloves in my kitchen, there will never be a better tool for removing hot mussels from their shells. I met a French chef once who winkled the first mussel out of its shell with a fork and then used the shell as tweezers, but he was so unbelievably cool that I couldn't dare try to emulate his insouciant deftness. Tweezers it is, then, and damn the reputational damage.

Use a slotted spoon to lift out the shellfish, shaking their juices back into the pan, tweeze out the meat and discard the shells. A combination of seawater and shellfish juice will have happily married with the wine in the bottom of the pan, the shallots and garlic will have given up their flavour and there's sure to be some sand, grit and bits of shell in the mix, too, so quickly pass the lot through a fine sieve and return to the pan. Now you can turn up the heat and begin reducing the liquid. It's difficult to judge how much you'll need to do this, but there's a clue in the smells coming off as it boils. I usually reckon things are done when the smell becomes maddeningly delicious, at which point, with the liquid still boiling hard, I add a large glug of olive oil.

When the oil hits the boiling liquid it's immediately dispersed into an emulsion (effectively a creamy sauce), which is why this phase is essential when cooking shellfish for pasta. You can, if you prefer, add a shot of whipping cream instead of the oil. Chefs prefer whipping to double cream because it doesn't split and it can be reduced by simmering, giving a better chance to get the consistency exactly correct.

While the sauce is getting towards perfect, sear both sides of a thick slice of sourdough in a dry pan.

You'll need to check the seasoning of the sauce before finishing. There will be plenty of salt in the reduced juices, but cream or oil tend to work against it, so don't ever be afraid to add more. A grind of black pepper wouldn't go amiss, and you might even consider some minced fresh chilli. Once perfectly seasoned, pour the shellfish back into the sauce and briefly stir it through to coat and reheat. At the very last moment, stir a handful of finely chopped fresh parsley or chervil through the shellfish and sauce before ladling it over your toast.

The principle of this inversion – of putting the bread under the dish instead of using it to clean up afterwards – is simple, but the results are sublime. One could argue that a steaming bowl of pasta or a bucket of *moules* in the middle of the table is a more convivial form of presentation, more public and gregarious, but for a more intimate meal or when dining solo, a bit of toast supplies the better medium.

Mushrooms on Toast

If shellfish are not for you, and I can see there may be reasons why, then mushrooms can be just as impressive. The best foods on toast are those with strong flavours and plenty of rich, oily juices to soak into the bread – even those with a gravy-like sauce. Mushrooms are excellent for this treatment. Mushroom flesh is basically a watery sponge. If you understand this, then most of the arcana about cooking them will immediately fall into place.

Cut some large mushrooms into thick slices, then throw them into a very hot dry pan and listen to them scream. No… I'm quite serious. You can 'fry' mushrooms in oil or butter, but that just seals the exterior. This is a better way. The noise the mushrooms emit is not protest but a near-explosive release of steam. They actually whistle as the water in them boils off. The steam forms a kind of cushion that stops the mushrooms sticking to the pan, although this is not a huge issue, because the scorched stuff that sticks just adds flavour to the eventual dish.

Shuggle the mushrooms about in the pan a bit and then, keeping the heat high, clap on a lid – a glass one is great if you have it because the next bit is instructive to watch. The mushroom pieces will continue to give off steam, some of which will condense on the lid and drop back down over them. It's an assault from all sides on the poor little fungi. They effectively give up all their juices and moisture and are cooked in them.

Once the pieces have become small and dark, remove the lid, lower the temperature a little and continue boiling off any remaining moisture. Keep stirring and scraping so that no bits stuck to the pan – the 'fond' – are left behind. When the pan is dry, the mushrooms are ready for you. They've been parched and cooked and will now absorb absolutely anything you offer them. Pour wine into the hot pan and they'll rehydrate themselves with wine. I love rehydrating myself with wine, too, but it does suck up a lot of unreduced booze. If you want a subtler effect, remove the mushrooms with a slotted spoon and reduce the wine first, deglazing the pan of its mushroomy fond.

So strong is the mushroom's thirst in this condition that it can be persuaded to suck up all kinds of useful fluids. Try a shot of mushroom ketchup, or you can even double down and use water you've used to soak dried porcini. We're kidding ourselves here, though; dancing around the obvious and brilliant truth: mushrooms will suck up butter. In quite surprising quantities. They become fat and astonishingly rich and this is the effect we're going for. Throw in a generous knob of unsalted, watch it melt and disappear… then do it again.

Eventually you'll have plump slices with a glaze of butter, at which point you can, if you wish, throw in a handful of chopped parsley, and a squeeze of lemon as an antiscorbutic and to cut the richness. You could also add a shot of cream and a really enthusiastic grinding of black pepper. Not just to mimsily 'season', you understand, but to the point that the pepper is actually behaving as a spice, adding fruity grace notes as well as heat. Either the herby butter or the pepper cream will soak superbly into a thick slice of white bread, toasted on both sides in a dry pan.

Scrambled Eggs

It is said that chefs who want to try out the skills of a new recruit will set them 'the omelette test', and it's true that making a good omelette will display many of the manual skills a good chef will need: the understanding of fire, swiftness of hand with the pan, an understanding of how egg behaves in the presence of heat and a degree of earned experience. The omelette is a good test of skill, but it is nothing compared with the creation of perfect scrambled eggs. An omelette might prove you're a worthy chef, but successful scrambling proves you are a fine human being, a noble and trustworthy character and an all-round good egg.

Scrambled eggs are, without possibility of doubt, the finest thing you can put on a piece of toast. These are not the horrid, rubbery strands in egg-water that sometimes get passed for scrambled eggs at a breakfast buffet, but something entirely more noble – a dish made in small quantities for yourself or a friend that requires so much attention that it implies at the very least deep affection and, more usually, unconditional love. You can't really say that about a bowl of muesli.

Scrambled eggs sit well on sourdough but can be equally sumptuous on a slice of nutty, malty brown bread. There are people, I'm sure, who have the agility of mind and body to handle toasting in parallel to the scrambling, but I confess that it's beyond me, and that's what's so charming about the process. You need someone else 'on the toast' if you're to devote enough attention to the eggs. You've got to love and trust that person, and you've got to have enough natural physical synchronicity and ease of communication with them to arrive at the table with your two parts of the dish simultaneously.

Crack five eggs into a bowl and beat them loosely with a fork. You'll need to add a pinch of salt and some ground white pepper. I know that since the '80s we've been forbidden to use the white stuff in favour of 'freshly ground black pepper', but chefs have always kept the secret… white pepper is more complex, more fragrant, more interesting and doesn't leave black bits in your teeth or besmirch the finish of a light sauce. This is refined, delicate, romantic breakfast cooking… we don't want besmirching… and we definitely don't want black bits in our teeth.

Take a thick slice off the end of your pat of unsalted butter, cut it into neat little cubes and arrange them on a saucer next to the stove. Keep your partner informed of your progress at all times – they will need to judge the correct point at which to drop the bread into the hot maw of the toaster.

Add a very little unsalted butter to the bottom of a small, non-stick saucepan and pour in your eggs. Begin to stir immediately with one of those silicone spatula/scraper jobs.

Purists will, by now, be shrieking in protest. 'Non-stick pans are unprofessional, they're hopeless at high temperatures, and silicone spatulas melt!' Both statements are completely correct… and it doesn't matter one jot, because you must have a non-stick saucepan and a silicone spatula *just* for making scrambled eggs. For no other purpose. Not for simmering milk for a late-night cardamom hot chocolate, nor for finishing a sorrel sauce for your barely poached salmon. No. Other. Purpose. Excessive heat will damage both items and, on the morning you need them most, you'll find your eggs sticking to a saucepan that's shedding its Teflon like an estate agent's dandruff, with a spatula as thwart and deformed as the mind of… well, an estate agent with dandruff. Your egg equipment will never experience extreme heat and will be with you much longer than any human relationship.

Stir the eggs gently but with purpose. No element of egg should adhere to the side or bottom of the pan for more than two turns of the spatula. Watch in increasing delight as the egg begins first to set and then form curds. In your stirring, swipe occasionally across the bottom of the pan and notice the speed with which the liquid egg flows back to cover the base. This is the unmistakable portent of perfection, for the very second the egg doesn't flow back to cover the base, you whip the pan from the heat, pour in the cubes of cold butter and beat as energetically as you can until it is melted and consumed by the eggs. The reduction in heat will immediately stop the eggs coagulating and they will combine with the fluid elements in suspension like an enriched custard and… oh, c'mon! BUTTER!

As you turn from the stove your partner will have the toast ready on two plates. Seared precisely, either naked or liberally smeared with further butter, to your preference. Share out the eggs, eat and, as long as someone remembered to put the coffee on, bask in your union.

Herring Roes

Noble though the eggs of a chicken are, they are by no means the only ova that benefit from a bed of toast. Herring roes are… well, let's say, 'it's complicated'. Go to a decent fishmonger in the spring or early summer[15] and you'll see them in tubs; flaccid, pink sacs with the texture of a dropped blancmange. The fishmonger will tell you that they are the reproductive part of a herring and will blithely assert that they contain 'eggs'. This is only correct about half of the time. As with most aquatic creatures, sexual contact between herring is indiscriminate. The females hose their eggs all over the shop and the males follow, spending their seed like Onan. Both sexes produce similar quantities of gametes, so the number can eventually stack up and there is very little to distinguish one from the other.

Fishmongers, perhaps unfairly, have concluded that 'delicious fish sperm' isn't exactly going to fly off the slab, so obfuscation and creative euphemism have been employed.[16] Ask the fishmonger very directly and he may be able to tell you if his roes are indeed 'hard roe' (female), 'soft roes'/'milt' (male) or a racy mixture of the two. Just so you know, FYI, etc.

In their raw state, roes are messy to handle, but dropped into hot water for a swift poach, they tighten up into something approximating texturally to chicken livers. Dry them off on kitchen paper, then roll them in seasoned flour. You can make this as simple or as complicated as you like: pepper and salt will allow the subtle flavour of the roe to play out in full, whereas the more traditional and robust 'devilling' flavours will perhaps make more of a feature out of the texture. There are as many recipes for seasoned flour as there are cooks, but you could say the devilling's in the detail. Hot cayenne pepper and English mustard powder are traditional, but you can add smoked paprika, Old Bay Seasoning or a pinch of your favourite curry powder. The important thing, as well as the bite of the spice, is that there's plenty of flour to crisp up when frying in butter.

---

[15] Or other times of the year if he's an enthusiast for the deep freeze. Roes don't really degrade much in freezing.
[16] Most people don't give too much thought to fish fornication, but not, apparently, American songwriter Cole Porter (1891–64) whose famous lyric 'Let's Do It' is a litany of piscine hanky-panky. He manages to squeeze in mentions of oysters, clams, jellyfish, eels, shad, soles and even goldfish, all freely copulating.

The loveliest thing about roes is the contrast between the crispy crust and the creamy, almost liquid contents, combining in each mouthful. Toast is the vehicle that transfers them to the mouth and catches the drips. For maximum crispness, be generous with the flour and fry in clarified butter, or even ghee if you appreciate that extra fermented tang. With the milk solids removed, clarified butter can reach stonking temperatures without burning or becoming bitter, so you can really crank up the heat.

If your butter is hot enough it shouldn't take more than a few seconds to turn the roe's dusty coating into a tanned, crunchy shell, fully cooked with all the flavours of butter and caramelisation balancing the spice.

Bruschetta

Though I hymn in praise of the many advantages of toasted bread for mopping up juices and transporting toppings, few of us think of its useful abrasive qualities. I'm not suggesting for a moment that you use a bit of grilled ciabatta to get your window frames ready for a gloss coat or that you employ a seedy organic granary to exfoliate your dry patches, but toast can do something remarkable to garlic.

Consider, for a moment, the amount of effort cooks put into learning how to get garlic into a dish. We trouble ourselves about garlic presses. Are they unprofessional? Elizabeth David certainly thought so. We learn to chop garlic finely or crush it with salt with the side of our knife blade. Aficionados dote on the scene in *Goodfellas* where Paulie shaves a clove of garlic with a razor blade, and many of us have bought high-tech, laser-cut Microplane graters that shred garlic into a sauce almost as efficiently as they shred our fingers. But none of this is necessary with toast.

Give it a try. Take a peeled clove and rub it across the surface of even the most delicate, most anaemically toasted slice and you will be amazed at the effect. You're expecting the tough little clove to tear up the toast, but quite the opposite happens. The bread just *eats* the garlic. It wears it away faster than the sharpest grater, reducing it to liquid that immediately soaks in. You have to take it carefully or within a few strokes a small slice will have absorbed an entire raw clove and you won't feel comfortable getting into a lift with anyone for a month.

This is the fundamental principle behind bruschetta in Italy and *pa amb oli* in Catalonia. The very simplest peasant staple of unsalted, often stale bread can be enriched to become one of the most luxurious foods on the planet with the local ingredients of garlic, oil and salt. Most Italians will cheerfully stab you in the neck if you imply that their olive oil could be improved upon, but some, nonetheless, apply the oil with a 'brush' made of fresh rosemary – doing so is rather gilding the gingerbread, though. Really you just need to rub on the garlic, pinch on a little salt and then hose on the oil like a profligate Baptist. Some will soak in, some will sit on the surface and some will run down your arm, but it's only then that you know you've got things right.

It is but a short and quite natural step from *pa amb oli* to the princely *pa amb tomàquet* (or *pan con tomate*). I'd like to think that the most authentic version of this is when a Mallorcan has toasted her bread, rubbed on the garlic, poured on the oil and then reaches to a nearby vine and plucks a just-about-to-be-overripe tomato and smooshes it into the bread. This would probably be the ideal, with the sharp juices soaking into the bread and marrying perfectly with the fruity oil.

To my eternal regret, I rarely have spectacularly fresh tomatoes to hand, so I usually have to use other common tricks to improve the ones I have. Most supermarket tomatoes in the UK seem to have thick and indigestible skins. The fastest way to deal with these is to peel them, which, before you roll your eyes and laugh at the very thought of such frippery, is actually very easy. You just cut a cross in the skin at the bottom of the tomato and pour boiling water over it. That's it. It takes seconds. The shock of the boiling water shrinks the skin, the cross in the bottom will elongate into long fissures and you can take the skin straight off in four pieces.

Conventional wisdom says you shouldn't keep tomatoes in the fridge, and that's quite true for fresh ones, but once they've been peeled, they're better preserved by the cold. The tendency of the fridge to dry things out works to your advantage, concentrating the flavour of the tomato. There are varying beliefs around how the tomato should be applied to the bread. Some like to crush it; some halve it, take out seeds and pulp and finely chop the flesh. For me, the way the juices soak into the bread is the whole point, so I just roughly chop the whole thing, seeds and all, salt it well and scoop it onto my oiled and garlicked slice.

A peeled tomato that's been stored in the fridge has a texture strangely similar to that from a tin, which leads us inexorably down a dark and embarrassing side alley, to the bizarre British favourite of 'tinned tomatoes on toast'.

Boy, this is an odd one. It's got a definite feeling of post-war austerity about it; of a surplus in some far reach of the Empire being preserved and sent back to miserable, grey Blighty and being encouraged by government as a prophylactic treatment for scurvy. Like those sardines on toast, it's got a touch of the Patrick Hamilton, heated-on-a-gas-ring about it. In fact, it's such a grim urban folk recipe that it's never, as far as I can find, been written down.

The thing is, though, that however forgotten, neglected and derided they might be, tinned tomatoes on toast are delicious – particularly if you can get a can of San Marzano tomatoes from a specialist Italian deli. San Marzanos are a DOP-certified variety, grown on the slopes of Mount Etna in volcanic soil enriched with crushed seashells. Connoisseurs say you can detect the faintest hint of the sea in them. I'd say that was probably bollocks, but they are the tomatoes that are used, with no further cooking, on the finest and most rigorously authentic pizzas in Naples. Maybe, then, it's not such a crazy idea to pour some over a lovely bit of sourdough toast and flash them under the grill.

Fried Bread

In the strict liturgical hierarchy of the British fry-up, fried bread is a step up from toast. Toast treats bread to the Maillard reaction and then, if served correctly, can absorb plenty of melted fat – but actually frying the bread, adding the fat before putting it onto the hotplate, jacks things up a level. And it's not just the spatula jockey in a greasy spoon, flashing his slice in the hot bacon grease, who thinks this. A thin slice of brioche, slid into hot, clarified butter, is rich and refined enough to be a bed for foie gras in the most starry of restaurants. Bread can be fried until shatteringly crisp and dry (think good croutons) or fried blonde in duck fat and tossed onto a frisée salad – not greasy, not heavy, but somehow sublimated; rendered more airy by the process.

At the other end of the spectrum, bread can soak up colossal amounts of fat. There's a point during the making of a bacon sandwich at which the most responsible cook will rub the bread around the inside of the frying pan so that not a drop of the precious chrism will 'go to waste'. You can get a bacon roll in a paper bag to take away, but if the bag hasn't gone transparent from the grease by the time you get to the door, take it back to the counter and complain.

A well-shaped slice of simple, white bread looks so enticing when lightly fried that it appeals to restaurant chefs almost as a canvas. In Italy, these appear as *crostini*; in Spain, it might feature as *pan frito*; and in restaurants anywhere else around the globe where a chef is looking for ideas and has spare bread, they'd pop up as canapés or starters. I can't insult you by suggesting recipes for something as simple as this. Anything can be added, from anchovies to mashed raw peas and crumbled feta, *caponata* to peanut butter, potted shrimp to guacamole. The important thing to remember, though, is that all of these are better than 'toppings on toast'. That creamy, fatty unctuousness that frying brings underlays everything and ennobles it, and therefore, you must choose your frying medium with as much care as you choose what will go on top.

Fried bread is a powerful thing for me, as my favourite recipes for it are rooted deep in my childhood. We were not wealthy when I was small. I imagine that my brother and sister and I were probably very fussy and I don't remember the kitchen facilities looking much like the Sunday supplements. Mum would take a slice of white packaged bread – medium-sliced Sunblest, as I recall, was the family favourite, with red and white wax paper rather than the blue and white of the luxurious thick sliced – and fry it in bacon fat or lard. This was cut into quarters, to better fit our greedy pie-holes, and topped with a mound of leftover mashed potato. The crowning garnish to this glorious canapé was to stick your fat little thumb into the top of the potato and then fill the hole with ketchup (see page 51).

One-eyed Egyptians

Another juvenile, fried-bread delight from my childhood was one of those odd ideas that crops up pretty much wherever there's a mum at the stove and kids to demand treats. Everyone has different names for this: you will have your own and I'm prepared to accept that your mum did them best. We called them one-eyed Egyptians, but nobody knows why and I'm sure your name is better.

Take a single slice of bread and, using a small wine glass or a biscuit cutter, cut a hole out of the centre. In butter or bacon fat, fry one side of the slice and the cut-out disc. Flip both, add a dot more fat or butter to the centre of the hole and then crack an egg in. After a few seconds, lower the heat, season the top of the egg with salt and pepper and put a lid over the pan.

Lift the lid occasionally to check how the egg is setting, and once it starts to look right, gently lift the edge of the bread to ensure it's brown and not burned. I usually remove the lid towards the end to slow down the cooking and allow steam to escape so that the bread can stay crisp.

Lift your Egyptian onto a plate with a wide spatula, being careful not to rupture the underside of the egg. Finally, slice the crisp, fried disc in half and apply to the egg as an amusing garnish. I've just called Mum who's confirmed that arranging them 'like little ears' is most likely to delight me.

Mince on Toast

Recently, in a very fashionable bar somewhere in New York, a young man with a beard offered me a 'loose meat, smash burger'. There was, as there always is, a little tableside narrative about the earnest authenticity of it, how the ground beef was seared on the plancha and served, not in a bun, but on a griddled slice of their house sourdough. It was all very charming... but, god, it made me yearn for the real thing.

I'm sure that, back in the day, Mum just browned some minced meat, stirred in some Bisto gravy and poured it onto a fried slice, but this homely combination has so much potential. Over the years, it's become the greasy peak of my home-cooking repertoire.

Start with the mince. Everyone knows by now that cheap cuts are tastier and that fat carries flavour, so, counterintuitively, the cheapest grade of supermarket beef mince is not to be scorned. It's full of all the tastiest and toughest extremities and has a good, high fat percentage. But if you want the reassurance of control, get your butcher to help you choose some good, complex, fatty brisket, a quantity of chuck and maybe some short rib, and ask him to mince it for you. It's the kind of combination you'd want for a very authentic burger, but fattier.

Most recipes start with firm instructions to 'brown' the mince. This is based on the idea that searing the surface of each individual meaty grain will seal the juices inside. It's a principle that has long been disproved about steaks, so it's time we questioned it for mince. Minced meat in its own gravy should, by the time it's been properly cooked, be a near-homogenous slurry, with the meat just supplying the barest hint of granular texture.

If all the juice leaches out into the gravy, it will only be a good thing. The best way, in this case, to brown the mince is to start it in a pan, on a high heat with a small quantity of water. The water helps to break the mince up completely and gives an initial 'steaming' that renders out fat and some proteins.

In less than a minute, you should have found that the water has boiled off and the completely lump-free, lightly steamed mince is now frying in its own fat, the proteins helping to form the Maillard crust that gives grilled meat its best umami flavour. If you fancy adding an alcohol to your flavouring, you can use it instead of water. White wine is a modest, delicate addition; port would not be insane; Madeira sublime.

Cook the mince hard to really build the flavours up and you should end up with dry, free-flowing and granular cooked meat. Now add enough strong chicken stock to cover the mince, reduce the heat to the barest simmer and step away. Forget about it for a good half hour before briefly revisiting to top the stock back up and cover the mince again. Forget everything you've ever learned about keeping good meat rare. This is not a steak or a poncey burger. This is effectively a thick beef gravy with a very carefully managed textural addition.

Season to taste, initially with salt and pepper, but then pause for a moment of quiet contemplation. Where do you want to go next? A tiny shot of sriracha sauce will subtly perk things up, more sriracha will make it properly hot (though that's not really to my particular taste). A touch of tomato purée is no bad thing... little enough that things don't go fully Italian, but enough to boost the umami... a truly fearless cook might even try a shot of tomato ketchup – though I'm not keen on the sweetness it adds. Soy sauce is never wrong, either, but for me there's one secret ingredient that really helps the whole thing achieve launch velocity. I religiously hoard the vinegar from jars of pickled walnuts – indeed, I've been known to replenish my stock by deliberately cooking beef and pickled walnut pies, just to have another season's worth of the precious fluid. Just a few drops of this imparts a combination of traditional English spicing that's quite similar to Worcestershire sauce but with the added acetic kick of vinegar, acting as what the French refer to as a *gastrique*... the shot of sour that's unusual in British recipes but which stimulates the taste buds.

Proper mince and gravy is, to use the formal term, 'runny'. The Italians bang on endlessly about how the texture of risotto should be 'pourable' and that it should pool and puddle on the plate. In exactly the same way, mince should end up as a naturally thick, gelatinised gravy, with small, soft grains of flavourful meat suspended in it. If your mince is too granular, the pieces chewy or the liquid too clear and separate, it's not proper, because the point of the bread is to soak up all that thick, gravy amazingness.

Choose a substantial white bread, doughy and with a proper crust – bloomer or split tin would be right – and cut a slice about two centimetres (almost an inch thick). Allow it to stand for an hour or two so that the outer surface is dry and a little stale. Moist bread takes extra heat in the pan to drive off steam, so it won't crisp as nicely when fried. Start by grilling the bread in a dry pan, flipping it until both sides have begun to crisp but not colour, then drop some dripping into the pan and fry the bread until both sides are golden brown. Transfer the fried slice to a place, mound the mince on top of the bread and serve. As you cut through the slice and allow the gravy to soak the soft heart of the bread, consider how brilliantly this has transformed the very cheapest of butcher's meat into something nourishing, delicious and emotionally fortifying by the simple addition of time, effort… and bread.

Prawn Toast

It's not entirely clear where sesame prawn toast originated. It's a popular starter in British–Chinese restaurants and a feature of *dim sum* and *yum cha* spreads both here and in the US and Australia. What's difficult is working out at what point the impressive repertoire of Chinese ingredients was supplemented by crap white bread. It first appears on menus around a hundred years ago in Guangzhou, near the international entrepôts of Hong Kong and Macau. It's called *hatosi* in Cantonese, where *ha* means 'shrimp' and *tosi* means 'toast' – again, a loan word from English. It's reasonable to assume, therefore, that the British, as colonisers, were at least partially responsible.

Though there are various breads in Cantonese cuisine, I can't help feeling that prawn toast has always been reliant on the poor quality of manufactured western-style loaves for its unique appeal. The bread needs to be dense, a little sweet so that it takes well to deep-frying and not absorbent enough to be greasy while caramelising nicely from the heat. As a popular and democratic snack around the world, it's logical that prawn toast shouldn't taste too fishy and, in essence, the combination is a textural variation on neat fried bread... and I mean that in the very best way.

To make some, put prawns, an egg white, some salt, spring onions, a little fresh ginger and a shot of light soy into a blender. Blitz the whole lot to a paste as you would if making prawn or fish balls or cakes. You could, if you wish, invest in the very highest-quality prawns and chop them more coarsely to retain the integrity of your luxury ingredient, but you'd be missing the point. You could add a splash of *nam pla* fish sauce or maybe a squirt of sriracha for hipness, but d'you know what? Don't.

You'll need plain, white packaged sliced bread and you could possibly cut off the crusts to create more elegant canapés, but this would also be missing a trick, because part of the joy is the extra crunch of the fried crust. There's a reason they've evolved to be triangles in Chinese restaurants.

Smear on a good thick layer of the prawn paste, smoothing the edges down to meet the bread perfectly and creating a regular domed shape. The prawns will set to an absolutely homogenous texture that's just short of rubbery and you don't want them to detach from the toast when frying. Once you've used up all your paste, sprinkle the toasts with sesame seeds. Again, you could get creative with a mixture of black and white seeds... but when did you ever see *that* in a Chinese restaurant?

Drop the toast into a deep-fat fryer. When cooked, drain on kitchen paper, wait a few moments for them to cool and then bite into them – they will be the best prawn toasts you have ever tasted. Not because of the quality of your seafood or your relationship with your supplier, not because you hand baked the bread, not even because you invested in a particularly high-quality oil. It'll be the best because this simply glorious combination has evolved from the tastes of millions of diners across the world, and is unimprovable in any way, save for serving it spankingly fresh from the fryer.

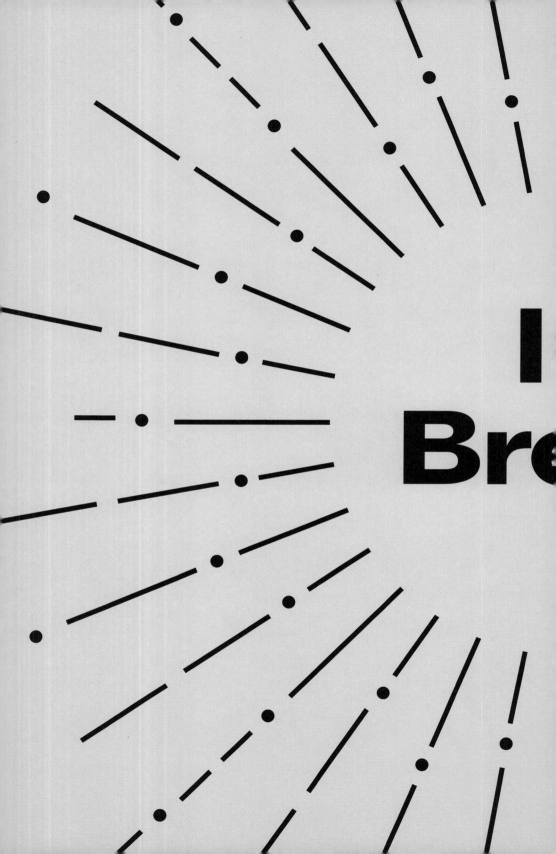

I
Bre

Meat Paste and Matpakke

To say that my grandfather was an unadventurous eater would be a tremendous understatement. He was, in the vernacular of the day, a 'martyr to his dicky tummy' and, throughout his life, whenever a food gave him 'the pip' he'd expunge it from his repertoire forever. By the time he died, he was surviving entirely on a diet of weak tea and sandwiches – supermarket sliced bread and Shippam's Beef Spread.

Looking back, there are two reasons for this. Pop Ron's was not a generation that bothered their doctors lightly, so he'd never have received an early diagnosis of gastric reflux, IBS, diverticulitis or Crohn's disease. It was just the sort of thing one lived with.

He was also part of the worst generation in British history for eating. He was born in a Welsh mining village and as a child watched it destroyed by the Depression. He spent the war as an intelligence officer, debriefing young Canadian bomber crews who'd been shot to pieces over Germany, then spent the rest of his working life as the headmaster of an underfunded state school in a devastated urban sink. His generation didn't care for food much and in his case this was exacerbated by an entirely justifiable and deep-seated anhedonia.

I, too, in a small way, ended up on the family 'paste diet'. I'd like to think it was a subconscious act of solidarity with the old man but, truth be told, it was the appalling and intractable conservatism of childhood that meant, through my thirteenth and fourteenth years, I refused almost every food except white bread and Shippam's Sardine & Tomato Paste.

Meat and fish pastes are still around. They exist in a weird little time warp of forgotten but much-loved Victorian prepared foods along with corned beef, custard powder and tinned meat pies. We should be thinking fondly of them: potted ox cheek, brown shrimp, rabbit and haddock pepper the menus of every 'modern British' restaurant in the country. They are on-trend signifiers of thrift and authenticity. We should even doff our hats to the cooking method. Pastes are actually cooked inside those little pop-top jars – the same way as the foie gras or rillettes we disloyally rush to buy on trips to French supermarkets.

Of course, you probably won't be aware of meat paste. Why should you be? It lives on the 'granny shelf' of the supermarket. Right down there at the bottom, just before the pet food, along with the tinned mince, the Camp Coffee and the last bottle of gravy browning. You won't see it unless you're moving very slowly, dragging a trolley, bent double with arthritis and trying to work out how to live on the last eight pence of your pension. If you're a straight-backed shopper of average height, your eyeline will be occupied by overpackaged premium mueslis and jars of artichoke hearts preserved in olive oil – you're not meant to notice the soul-sapping depressiveness of the knee-height shelves.

But recently I did. I don't know what made me look down, but there it was, a little tray of the store's own-brand pastes, and I realised that those two flavours that had run like veins through my childhood hadn't passed my lips in thirty years. It seemed an amazing opportunity. I instantly recalled the bland suavity of the beef paste and, though nobody knew what it was back then, the genuinely umami jolt of the sardine and tomatoes. How could I resist?

I bought a special loaf for the taste test. I was looking forward to trying these flavours again, expecting some Proustian surge of emotional recognition. I wanted something close-textured and very white to smear them on – something that would replicate the bread I remembered.

The beef paste had a smell I didn't remember… a non-specific meatiness on the cat food spectrum with a light descant of metallic notes. The taste failed to live up even to that promise, distinguished by nothing but its utter blandness, and I realised that I'd laid it on in a thick curl like some poncey paté. Pop would have spread it thin enough to see the bread through it, then put three-quarters of the jar back in the fridge for the rest of the week. Looking at the ingredients I noted that beef paste now features chicken and chicken skin. It probably did then, too, but now I feel I can actually taste it.

The sardine and tomato paste still smelled as unholy as it ever did. It would incubate in a Tupperware lunchbox throughout a morning of double physics until it smelled like an abandoned fishing smack. Much like Marmite, though, eating it was about sensation more than flavour; a brutal mouth mugging that was somehow fixed in my teenage mind as enjoyable. Now it sat on the bread, the consistency of baby poop and – there's no other word for it – stank. A mouthful produced just an evanescent whiff of recollection. The ingredients list features mackerel in large proportions. I screwed the lids back on and consigned the lot to the bin. It was then that I noticed that the lids of the jars still bear the same legend they did then: 'reject if centre can be depressed', which, under the circumstances, seemed prophetic wisdom.

Just Enough Lunch

I felt guilty about my 'sandwich conservatism' for many silent years, then, quite recently, two new ideas came to my attention. The first came in the form of a poll of 2,000 people in 2017 by the New Covent Garden Soup Co., which found that one in six people had eaten the same lunch every day for at least two years. The same poll revealed that 77 per cent of workers had eaten the same lunch every day for the past nine months. This was astonishing stuff. Perhaps I might dare believe that I was actually normal. Then, as the entire world started buying up scented candles and cashmere socks and banging on relentlessly about *hygge*, I found out about *matpakke* – the Norwegian packed lunch.

To understand *matpakke*, you first need to understand a little about *lagom*. In Sweden, *lagom* famously refers to a profound belief, at a culture-wide level, in the notion of 'sufficiency' – the correct or adequate amount – leading to a pursuit of balance and moderation in everything. In Norwegian, *lagom* has a subtly different meaning of 'fitting', 'proper' and 'reasonable' – perhaps a more moral interpretation.

Lagom is the motivating spirit in Norway's national packed lunch. It originated in a system of free school meals launched in 1932 called the Oslo Breakfast (requiring no cooking and supplied free to all – including bread, cheese, milk, half an orange and half an apple). It was simple, unembellished and, as it was a universal provision, proudly displayed an entirely non-competitive standard of adequacy. Rich kids couldn't get a better breakfast, poor ones wouldn't have a worse one. The food was precisely sufficient – the purest expression of *lagom*.

Today the noble ideals of the Oslo Breakfast persist in *matpakke*. During the state-mandated half-hour lunch break, every worker from floor sweeper to CEO will unwrap a wax-paper package containing two sandwiches and a piece of fruit. Being Norwegian, the sandwiches are open-faced and use a modest single slice of packaged bread each, so a specially manufactured sheet of greaseproof paper (*mellomleggspapir*) is placed between the sandwiches to separate them. The fillings are simple: cheese, ham, salami, liver paste or jam. It would, after all, be wrong to include any ostentatious condiments – it would be antisocial to produce something that was more pleasurable than that of your colleagues and, in fact, it would be kind of insulting if your lunch was more temptingly delicious than your neighbour's... if you 'looked forward to it' for any reason other than peckishness. I can't think of any other situation in the world where the driving imperative is for the food to be, well, *reassuringly dull*.

I can't adequately express how vindicated I feel by *matpakke*. My stubbornly narrowed choice of lunch as a boy wasn't lonely or mad; it was innovative, egalitarian and praiseworthy. It's probably time we thought like this a little more.

Have you ever dragged yourself from your desk, through rainy streets, stood frozen by indecision and guilt in front of a large 'grab-'n'-go'[17] fridge, plumped for the same awful, over-mayo'ed, troublingly moist, nine-month-shelf-life, gas-flushed monster sandwich as yesterday, then queued for ten minutes to be plundered of a fiver?

Have you never thought what a complete relief boring simplicity might be? Then you, too, my friend, have dreamed of *matpakke*.

[17] Are there any two-and-a-half words in the English language as depressing as these?

Sandwiches

If I had to choose a desert-island meal or a last request on Death Row, I can say, without having to ponder for too long, that it would be the sandwich. There's something honest and uncomplicated about the sandwich. At its simplest it's a lump or slice of something slipped between two bits of bread to facilitate its transit to the mouth. The story that it was invented by the Earl of Sandwich when he needed something he could eat quickly and cleanly without leaving the card table is almost certainly apocryphal, but, like all good origin myths, it makes so much sense that it no longer matters. The sandwich is the ultimate logical food, evolving automatically out of hunger, convenience and an absence of formality.

Americans have long understood the sandwich. There are counters in Manhattan where the combinations of fillings, seasonings, breads and condiments are so numerous and complex as to be, to all intents and purposes, infinite. At some Jewish delis, sandwiches containing stacks of sliced meats weighing up to a kilogram (more than two pounds) are served by legendarily surly staff. An inexperienced diner is confused as to whether they should try to eat it and fail, or set up a series of base camps and plan the assault over days. Cognoscenti ask for a doggy bag.

That being said, we in Britain could lay claim to be leaders in the world of sandwiches. According to the estimable British Sandwich & Food to Go Association, the first fully packaged, pre-made sandwich was sold by Marks & Spencer in 1985. Today, the UK's pre-made sandwich industry is by far the largest in Europe.

This should be exciting for sandwich lovers, but it's a more complex story than it at first seems. The same august body estimates that 43,000 tonnes of chicken, 16,000 tonnes of cheese, 15,000 tonnes of ham and 14,000 tonnes of egg are consumed by the sandwich industry each year yet, as we have already seen, we respond to this ridiculous display of choice and constant novelty by making the same selection every day, like children returning to a knackered old bear or blanket for comfort and security.

Once I could have wandered into any half-decent sandwich bar and ordered one to my exact taste; today, although I apparently have more choice than I've ever had before, it seems that I can't.

Boring Lunch

The pre-made sandwich is now such a complicated, multilayered and exotically flavoured thing that it's worth, just occasionally, reminding ourselves of the basics – the platonic archetypes of the sandwich world – and how, when done right, they can still be the very best.

In the British repertoire, cheese is the OG sandwich. An agricultural worker, lopping off a chunk of cheese with his pocketknife and sticking it in a piece of bread torn off a loaf, is an image that pre-dates the supposed invention of the sandwich in art and literature. And rightly so, because mature Cheddar on a thick slice of crusty white farmhouse bread is still something that transcends all attempts at commercial innovation.

Because it's the simplest combination, the details of each separate element become vitally important. The cheese doesn't need to be artisanal or particularly distinguished, but it has to be cheesy. Mild or medium Cheddars – what the supermarkets insist on primly rating as '1' or '2' strength – are 'textural' cheeses. Intentionally bland. Designed to provide a waxy layer of bulk in a mixed filling; to be grated and melted; to be gummed by small children and the weak-minded. Aged Cheddars, like people, get salty, sour and a hell of a lot more interesting. They are also drier, which is why the choice of butter is key. Both salted and unsalted butter work well but should be chosen depending on the saltiness of the cheese and should be laid on thick.

In commercial sandwich making, butter is what's called a 'barrier'. It's used to waterproof the bread and stop the juice of tomatoes or other wet fillings from soaking into the bread and making the sandwich soggy.

Depressing, isn't it? Noble butter reduced to a kind of greasy sealant. In a cheese sandwich, though, the butter really matters. It isn't applied in a coy smear to prevent the undesirable mingling of incompatible elements, but as a thick layer; a vital constituent in what the professionals would doubtless term the 'flavour profile'.

Usually, the bread should be white. Commercial white bread is quite sweet, and a lovely counterbalance to the salty/sour cheese, whereas a sourdough, though it looks better on Instagram, takes the entire sandwich too far into the sour end of the spectrum. I have a personal soft spot for a cheese roll that used to be served at the famous vegetarian restaurant Cranks. It was an early British artisanal loaf in the 'healthy bread' idiom of the time. Wholemeal flour, a good helping of sweetening malt, a handful of scouring seeds and a little molasses. It combined sweetness with nuttiness... not perhaps as rigorously, classically austere as it could have been, but picking up beautifully on the nutty notes in the emphatically rustic Cheddar. Bless them, but I suspect that back then they hadn't worked out that cheese wasn't necessarily fully veggie-compliant. More innocent days.

You can, of course, add to the cheese sandwich. A slice of raw onion has historical precedent as a 'relish', but I can't help feeling that if the sandwich needs perking up like that, it's either been poorly made or the diner has become jaded. Pickles are even worse... an extra, punchy layer of sweet and acetic flavour stamps all over the subtlety of the basic ingredients in combat boots. Don't get me wrong, cheese and pickle is a lovely combination in which the waxiness of the cheese leavens the punch of the pickle, but you can make one of those with a No. 1 or No. 2. Indeed, 'cheeseandpickle' is a sandwich filling in itself, in a whole different category.

When we speak of a 'cheese sandwich' today, we imagine the saddest, most minimal option on offer. Three miserable layers of over-processed, homogenised rubbish without distinguishing features, defined by all the things it could be but isn't. But a proper cheese sandwich gives infinite opportunity to blend and balance salt, sweet, sharp, sour and umami just as surely as a bowl of ramen or an exotic masala.

The French, perhaps predictably, understand this *faites simple* approach well. They revere the *jambon beurre* – the bestselling sandwich in France and one that makes best use of their high-standard baguettes. Note the name, though. It's not a 'ham baguette', it's a 'ham and butter'. Like our own, dear cheese sandwich, copious butter is a feature player.

A cheese sandwich is largely about flavour balancing, but in a *jambon beurre*, texture is brought into play. Once you've bitten through the crust, the main experience of a cheese sandwich is soft crumb. In a *jambon beurre*, by design, *every bite has crust*. The French are rightly proud of their crusty baguettes, and the ham, predominantly supplying saltiness, and the unsalted butter, providing an emollient mouthfeel, have evolved as the perfect balance to the crisp/sour outer casing.

There has to be something in this structural development because, when the British finally got round to formalising bread and cheese, it was as the 'ploughman's lunch': Cheddar cheese with a 'French stick' – British white bread in a baguette shape.

The sandwich is an admirable vehicle for proper philosophical and gastronomic analysis of good ingredients. Foie gras needs to be spread on brioche toast to be truly appreciated by privileged connoisseurs, but, at the other end of the social scale, the magnificent complexity of boiled crab can't really be enjoyed until it's wrangled from its bony matrix and smeared on triangles of brown bread. Preferably in bare feet and within yards of the ocean.

Recipes for the cucumber sandwich expend thousands of words on the precise seasoning of the vegetable and the choice of butter. You can stick some sliced cuke in white bread and cut the crusts off, but it's the grace notes that make it a masterpiece – and that's before you spend hours happily considering its cultural role as a class signifier, a social lubricant in novels and a music hall joke. The simplest sandwiches contain the most.

The Corned Beef Sando (CBS)

My personal favourite is a tinned corned beef sandwich on a medium-sliced split-tin loaf. For this you need a small-town bakery. They bake the loaves on site, but they also have a slicing machine. It's a unique combination that's worth seeking out because you'll have the precision of machine-made slices while the bread will be additive-free and fresh. The key to the entire sandwich is temperature. The bread and butter must be at room temperature while the corned beef is sliced straight from the fridge. Warm corned beef is delicious, but its texture is soft and greasy – when cold it has additional crack and pop. The single-ingredient sandwich is like a fine artist's economic line. It expresses a lot with what appears as minimum effort, and it concentrates the mind wonderfully.

I've always found it profoundly sad that the corned beef sandwich isn't better understood and therefore more honoured. It is as fulfilling and aesthetically perfect as any more fashionable sandwich… hell… if we could just get people to Instagram corned beef on white sliced the same way they do an artisanal *Katsu Sando* (see page 119), it could be just such an international phenomenon.[18] The corned beef sandwich can only ever be improved by one thing… a generous dressing of salad cream, whereupon it transcends the everyday ordinariness of its name; like a BLT it deserves its own acronym. Behold, then, the 'CBS'.

[18] After writing a sorrowful piece in a newspaper about how the British no longer appreciate their own great corned beef, I was thrilled to receive a message from a reader in Japan who told me that corned beef or *konbiifu* is avidly consumed there and even sold in the traditional 'trapezoidal' tins. Though post-war *konibiifu* was apparently made with horse meat, there is now a much coveted and luxurious Wagyu version.

IN BREAD

The Chip Butty

My great-grandfather had his name on the front of a chip shop on
Kingsland Road in Bristol. In a fairer world, it wouldn't have been there.
My great-grandmother inherited the place from her family, but it was the
way of the world back then that they should put her husband's name over
the door – John Chillcott, known as Jack. The building's been gone for
decades now, and all we have is a single photograph of him, taken in 1913,
blinking in the daylight outside the dark little emporium. My nan, his
daughter, could still remember the place – eating out of newspaper as a kid,
sitting up on the counter. She made the best chips I ever tasted – carefully
chosen potatoes, washed, cut, mysteriously dried under a tea towel in the
fridge, then fried twice in the 'chip pan'.

This pan was actually the bottom half of an old aluminium pressure
cooker, the size of a bucket and with a wire basket that, to my appalled
childish fascination, was usually set in a solid block of flecked ivory fat.
I don't think a day ever passed when the chip pan wasn't used, so there
was no need for anything as worryingly modern as refrigeration. The fat
was boiled up every day, constantly replenished by the melted scraps of
anything with a high lipid content, so it was a rich, characterful brew of
dripping, lard, possibly butter, oils and, lord be praised, any fat remaining
from the daily breakfast bacon.

My mother wasn't keen on chips. She was of the generation of new
women who wanted little to do with unhealthy, heavy, old-fashioned foods.
Dad, meanwhile, a diligent young insurance loss adjuster, seemed to come
home at least twice a week, shell-shocked from another chip-pan fire. These
happened all the time, in family kitchens just like ours, when the hot fat
boiled over, caught on the gas flame, ignited the 100 per cent man-made-
fibre net curtains and spread to the expanded polystyrene foam ceiling tiles.

Mum feared chips would eventually kill us all; Dad had actuarial figures
proving that chip fat would finish us all off even sooner. It just took one
small flare-up, quickly and correctly suppressed with a damp tea towel,
before Dad carried the entire apparatus to the bin. I must have been about
eight when we became a chipless house and I had to skulk to Nan's for a

regular fix. In hindsight, Nan's chips explain my entire life. They were so good I'd probably have eaten them with anything… even liver… but they were best in a chip butty.

No one has ever been able to explain why a chip butty is so good. It shouldn't be. I mean, it's so *minimal*. So zen-like in its simplicity. A chip is a potato. Just spud. And the only addition to it is some undistinguished fat, a bit of Maillard reaction and salt. Surely if you stick that between two slices of bland white bread with butter, there can be no way it can exceed the sum of its parts. It makes no sense! And yet… and yet.

I reviewed a restaurant in Trondheim once – a tremendous place with the most amazing food from their own farms. They were obsessives, with a fourteen-course tasting menu that changed every day. On the night I went there was a potato dish: a pancake made from a particular kind of potato grown on the farm; a potato that grew small in the hard, cold earth, which was stored to dry and ferment a little and cooked in an extraordinarily simple and traditional way to give the cleanest and most intense experience of potato possible. It was staggering. It didn't just 'taste of potato', all the sub-elements that combined to imply potato-ness were individually isolated and amplified.

Perhaps we lack the philosophical tools, the conceptual apparatus, to really comprehend how in a chip butty the bread binds the chips into the perfect mouthful; how the butter, melted by the hot chips, lubricates the mouth and floods the flavours out over the tongue and its receptors. A food scientist might call it mouthfeel; a philosopher might point to memories of childhood or even the transgressive nature of something so resolutely *un*-improving; a sentimental writer might find poetic nostalgia in it. Somewhere, I'm sure, there's a food critic prepared to take a Marxist perspective and say that it combines the simplest foods of the urban proletariat in a glorious 'fuck you' to the bourgeoisie. For me, like that potato pancake, the chip butty uses bread and butter to amplify all the things that make a chip a chip and presents them to your mouth in a way you can't fail to appreciate. I bet the Japanese have a word for it.

The Crisp Sandwich

There are some foods – incredibly popular favourites – that actually don't have recipes. I know… that sounds odd. But consider this: if you go online and search 'recipe chilli con carne', your screen will fill with hundreds of thousands of variations, tweaks, twists and 'takes'. You will also learn, within a few clicks, that there is no 'original', there is no master recipe… in fact, nobody in Mexico would even call it 'chilli con carne'. I lack the correct ontological terminology for something that weird. It's an idea, a concept, commonly held by about half the population of the world, none of whom will ever agree on what actually constitutes it. The Americans have lifted a term, 'foodways', from the jargon of folklore research, so perhaps that's appropriate to the phenomenon of the crisp sandwich.

I confess that, for many years, the idea of a crisp sandwich simply appalled me. There is nothing inherently wrong about the combination of flavours – a crisp sandwich, after all, can't taste much different to a chip butty – but it was the textural challenge I couldn't face. Soft bread, a soft filling and a flavoured crisp seemed to be too outrageous a combination. Then, one day, appearing on the panel of a radio show about food, I shared my reservations with a live audience of about 300 people who, not to put too fine a point on it, howled me down. I had never before managed to provoke such ire… even when discussing the order in which to apply jam and clotted cream on a scone in Cornwall, or suggesting the inclusion of avocado in a stottie in Newcastle.

This was a way of eating I'd not encountered. It didn't feel part of my culture and I could find no written recipe or original source, so I began asking friends, colleagues and the great hive mind of Twitter. It immediately became clear that crisps in a sandwich raised partisan fury, innumerable ferociously defended combinations and a full set of prejudices. This was an authentic 'foodway'.

One highly respected food historian swore that the addition of crap crisps was the thing that made a cheap, gas-flushed sandwich edible in emergencies; a household-name celebrity chef endorsed only Hula Hoops in sandwiches; and the most significant food publisher of her generation recommended ham and cheese plus a particular brand of square crisps that tessellated elegantly between the layers.

Some swore that the crisps should remain whole until the first bite, some maintained that anyone who was not a complete barbarian would crush them until there were finger marks in the bread. Some claimed the superlative combination was salt and vinegar crisps with egg mayonnaise, others swore that combination was the only one that could induce a full gag reflex. What was amazing was the level of highly directed, white-hot passion around the idea, along with a complete inability of any two people to agree on how it should be done. I had to try it.

I bought the sandwich in a supermarket. It seemed to me that my personal issues with textural contrast would be most aggravated with a firm crisp and a sloppy filling, so I chose a simple cheese and ham, on brown bread with butter but no mustard or pickle. It seemed reasonable to expect the crisps to stand in for any condiment. Acquiring the crisps required more effort. I drove to three petrol stations before I found two bags of Salt & Vinegar Squares, and it took twenty minutes to persuade the attendant that I didn't require the free bucket of Diet Coke he offered with them.

I drove my ingredients to a quiet spot I know, behind some lock-up garages on the edge of town – it seemed the right sort of location – and began my experiment. I dissected the first half of the sandwich and crushed up the first bag of crisps before opening them. I had recently been fed a variety of *outré* toppings by chefs… crumblings of nuts, drifts of dried fish flakes, seaweed dusts and sprinklings of 'baconetti'… I figured crushed crisps could be classified that way and somehow out-manoeuvre my palate. It tasted pretty grim. Processed cheese and reassembled ham-trim overlaid with a redolence of chip fat. It was time for the real thing.

I separated the elements of the second sandwich and spread them on the passenger seat. I carefully tessellated the crisps between the ham and the cheese where the butter couldn't soften their crunch and gently reapplied the lid. I took a huge bite out of the corner and began to chew. The texture of the crisps gave context to the flavour, and the flavour really did go some way to redeeming the dire awfulness of the sandwich itself. Emboldened, I squished the remainder a little, leaving some discreet finger dents in the bread and listening with horror to a sound not unlike the bones of an ortolan when crushed by the tongue.

It was not appalling.

I texted my publisher with the details of my complex purchases and the authentically sleazy location of my experiment…

'You bought a supermarket sandwich?'

'Well… yes.'

'You dolt! You should have made your own.'

I think I have more work to do on the 'crisps in sandwiches foodway'. I understand that the failing is in myself. Somewhere, I know, there will be a combination that will entirely reset my attitudes. Until then, here is the short list of suggestions I keep in my notebook, which I know I must work through. I will, of course, be grateful to receive any more you might want to add.

- Cheese and onion crisps, Marmite, soft white roll.

- Pickled Onion Monster Munch, uncrushed. Ham baguette.

- Ready salted crisps in a bacon roll. No sauce.

- Plain Hula Hoops 'on anything'.

- Cheese and onion crisps in a cheese and onion sandwich (bread not specified).

- Crumbled Twiglets over mashed avocado on sourdough toast.

- Ready salted crisps, Nutella, white bread.

A Really Bad Sandwich

'Good' is an important word to food lovers. Writers of a certain era employ it like a verbal tic ('use good butter or a splash of good olive oil'); we read *The Good Food Guide* or *BBC Good Food Magazine*. 'Good' implies a simplicity: honest, straightforward 'rightness'. We define ourselves as aficionados by our willingness to seek out the good; through diligent selection of the best, most arcane or novel ingredients; by innovative preparation methods; and by the virulence with which we reject the bad. But, increasingly, I'm finding myself troubled by one devastating contradiction: by far the majority of the food out there that moves and inspires us as much as it nourishes is not 'good' at all. It's rubbish. If we're really to be food lovers, we have to acknowledge the importance of the *bad*.

For better or worse, most avowed food lovers don't know hunger. We might get a bit peckish occasionally, we might inflict a little austerity on ourselves when the trousers tighten, but we have the power to fix things before genuine, gnawing hunger bites. Hunger, though, rewrites our value system when it comes to 'good' or 'bad' food. To a starving man, any food is good, just because it's food.

The definition of 'badness' in food is so mutable, so specific to circumstance as to be functionally useless. The closer you get to an empirical definition of badness, the more it eludes you – Heisenberg's Uncertainty Rissole, if you will.

The uncertainty, though, is useful, enabling us to reposition bad food as it suits us. In the UK, for example, we are deeply conflicted about 'nursery food'. Nursery food is 'bad' because it's prepared in such a way as to remove any polarising tastes or flavours. It is neutered, dumbed-down and fed to the intellectually and sensually unformed. We use words like 'pap', 'pabulum' and 'baby food' pejoratively, and yet the emotions attached to childhood food are incredibly strong. It was served, usually, with more genuine, unconditional love than we'll ever experience again in our lives. Quality, even if we had the power to discern it, was immaterial, so is it any wonder that, in later life when we need to forgo adult cares and responsibilities and trigger deep feelings of being wanted and cared for, we call for dreadful 'comfort food'?

The mass-market hamburger is held up by food lovers as the exemplar of all things vile. The cheapest cuts of intensively farmed beef, ground to the point at which they can be eaten almost without chewing, served in a bun that is nothing like bread, with a thousand-year shelf life, under a shroud of 'cheese-like food product' and a sauce made of sugar syrup and nuclear waste. Yet, in one form or another, the burger is one of the most popular foods in the world.

As you read this, there are maybe half a million people worldwide chomping into a burger with no redeeming feature apart from a texture that doesn't challenge them to chew, and they're *loving* it. They think it's delicious. It warms and nourishes them. It makes them very, very happy. Your Big Mac, your Whopper or indeed your KFC, Taco Bell or Subway are *designed* to be the way they are based on the constant feedback of millions. I have no wish to get all Jeremy Bentham here, but it's bad food that provides the maximum amount of joy for the maximum number of people. When it comes to the gaiety of nations, fourteen-course tasting menus and 'nourish bowls' of kale and avocado don't even cause a flicker on the dial. By this logic, the Big Mac isn't 'bad' at all; it is, in the truest sense of the word, perfect.

Our attitude to bad food is in many ways peculiar to the UK. All across America, in even the most advanced and metropolitan cities, there are diners and tiny independent joints selling exactly the same 'special recipe' junk they've been slopping out since the 1930s. Cheesesteaks, sliders, barbecue, bowls of execrable 'chilli' and primordial split pea soup, all made from commodity ingredients and slammed onto the counter in front of delighted customers, from out-of-work welders to local political big shots. America has stayed true to its authentic 'bad food' in an unbroken line because it recognises bad food as a cultural asset and sees no shame in enjoying it. The UK diner equivalents have passed away unnoticed and unmourned, so today, if you want our national 'fried breakfast' in a big city, you're much more likely to get one painstakingly reconstructed from 'good' ingredients in a recently opened brunch venue than in an original greasy spoon. We, it seems, need to mediate our badness into good.

Consider, for a moment, the 'hangover breakfast'. Chefs, writers, critics – drinkers, all – attribute almost magical powers to the food they eat the morning after. The bacon roll with brown sauce, the mighty 'full English', a bowl of packet ramen or even what chef Thomasina Miers recently called the 'little red ambulance' – a can of Coke. It's a near-comprehensive list of the wrong, the forbidden and the scorned in the enlightened western diet, and yet to hear them speak, many of our most qualified commentators have at some point enjoyed these bad foods more than the outstanding stuff that fills their menus. Has alcohol destroyed their palates and their judgement? Not at all. Forget the Jesuitical gymnastics. Forget the strenuous post-rationalisation. Expert people say bad food is great… and they're right.

I've wondered for a long time how to properly demonstrate to enraged food lovers that their pursuit of perfection, their slavery to arcane and high-quality ingredients is but one quite boring facet of foodism – how to prove to them the importance of really bad food – and I realised that, in the end, the answer would have to be a recipe.

It's very important that we understand that this is not about irony. A goddamn down-home pulled pork BBQ sandwich made with rare-breed pork on a brioche bun is NOT bad food, it's irony. It's great food slumming. It's *nostalgie de la boue*, but it's not properly bad food.

To prove my point, the following recipe must use undistinguished ingredients, it must be prepared without cheffery, without tricks or trucs, without being 'transformed' by molecular voodoo, and finally it must be irresistible so that even the most exquisite of gourmands will wolf it down, without demur and unlubricated by irony, and weep with delight.

The Grilled Cheese

Grab yourself two slices of appalling bread. This must be the white packaged stuff from the corner shop. Processed bread is the way it is because most people like their bread soft and 'easy to eat', so it is barely baked. For a truly ghastly experiment, take the rest of your loaf and ball it up in your hands. Within seconds you'll have pushed all the air out of the slices and formed a large ball of undercooked dough. Packaged bread is made palatable by the addition of plenty of salt and usually a fair whack of sugar. Butter your two slices thickly.

You'll need two kinds of bad cheese. The French and Italians like cheeses that get runny and go off, but we thrifty Brits and the canny Americans favour the process of 'cheddaring'. The cheese is squeezed dry, salted, 'milled' through a machine and pushed out in blocks with a much-extended shelf life. Commodity block Cheddar is a fantastic way of utilising milk surpluses throughout the year. Grate a handful of the stuff, of if you want to go the whole nine yards, buy it pre-grated.

Add the Cheddar to a handful of grated bad mozzarella. Not the premium kind made from buffalo milk and packed in whey, but the solid, rubbery brick, made with cow's milk and devised mainly to make pizzas chewy without being too interestingly cheesy.

Mound a pile of the mixed cheeses on one buttered slice, top with the other, lay a cutting board on top and squeeze down. You will find that the assembly squishes pleasingly.

Slather the outside of the sandwich with mayonnaise. Avoid the low-fat versions – you want the kind they use by the litre in the commercial sandwich industry as a throat lubricant.

Fry the sandwich over a medium heat in a dry pan. The oil in the mayonnaise will provide the frying medium while the egg content, such as it is, will create a sort of omelettey crust. The sugar in the bread will caramelise a little and, when the cheesy centre is fully molten, flip the whole thing onto a plate to serve.

The 'Carpetbagger' Monte Cristo

In most matters of food and bread, the American diner or deli is
well ahead of us. While we were still cutting the crusts off triangular
cucumber sandwiches, they were creating the Reuben and the Muffuletta,
achievements far more impressive than merely putting men on the moon.
But with one particular creation they seem frankly to have run off the rails
– it is a sandwich that's become so confused and messy that it needs the
calming hand of the Old World to bring it back to the straight and narrow.
We're speaking of the Monte Cristo.

The original idea of a Monte Cristo seems pretty simple. It was a slice
of boiled ham and a slice of cheese, pulled from the grillman's *mise en
place*, slapped between two slices of bread and dipped in egg wash before
being fried gently in butter. It was a lovely thing. A warm, soft capsule
of ingredients, convenient to eat and with a faint hint of the noble
Italian *mozzarella in carrozza*. Suggestions, too, of the *croque-monsieur*,
but without Gallic faff or pretention. This, though, was not enough for
breakfast lovers of the US.

It made plenty of sense when cooks decided that the ham could be
replaced with sliced turkey, perhaps to create a pork-free option. It was
forgivable, too, when a pickle was introduced – who could deny the grill
monkey a little *jeu d'esprit* – but then things went crazy. Perhaps it was
an error in interpretation, but at some point, America got the idea that
'Monte Cristo' referred to the method of encasing, and they felt able to
go entirely off-piste with the contents. I've been served a fried chicken
and bacon jam Monte Cristo… a Vietnamese ham and liver spread
Monte Cristo from one well-intentioned fusionist… elsewhere avocados
have been introduced.

I'm by no means conservative in matters of taste, so perhaps these might
have survived, had it not been for one thing. One final, ridiculous step that
took a fine sandwich into the realm of the surreal. Americans are used to
serving 'French toast' for breakfast, made with a sweetened batter, enriched
with cream and topped with syrup or a dusting of cinnamon sugar. In all
these cases of bastardised Monte Cristos, the sandwich element was dipped
in sweetened French toast batter *and served with a sweet topping*!

Words almost fail me.

So, as a gift to the people of the United States, I'd like to offer a corrective recipe. Something that completely resets the standards. We need to get back to the absolute basics of what makes the Monte Cristo brilliant and then we can agree to forget all the other nonsense that's gone on in between. C'mon. This is America's hour of need.

That the bread must be soft and white shouldn't really be a matter for debate. We need something that's going to absorb some of the batter for richer flavour and better texture, so a decent commercial white sandwich loaf without any artisanal pretensions. This is, in engineering terms, a neutral matrix for the egg and a container for the ingredients, so socking great irregular air bubbles will just destroy the structural integrity. Cut a slab two-slices thick from the loaf.

In this particular recipe, the crust is useless to us. We don't need it to hold the bread together and its difference in texture will just create confusion; so slice it off and you should have on your board a rectangular cuboid of uninterrupted and entirely even, soft crumb.

Using the point of your knife, cut into one side of the bread to create a pocket. It should be a single cut, in such a way that you have two slices of equal thickness, still joined on three sides. Pause for a moment to admire your handiwork.[19]

Now you can very carefully introduce a little butter into the pocket and smear it around a bit, followed by a piece of smoked ham. You need something dry and properly flavourful… maybe a *Westfälischer Schinken*, the closest we can get in Europe to the secret and illegal 'country' hams of the Appalachians. Now we need cheese. It needs to be something that melts prettily and, if we're to follow our strategy here fully, it should be the only thing in the sandwich with a possibility of conveying sweetness. A Gruyère would do the trick, or a Comté if you're feeling cheeky. Slip that in alongside the ham. This is the time when, if you were some sort of

---

[19] I always think of this as a 'carpetbagger' Monte Cristo. Carpetbagger is a way of serving steak that is popular in Australia and the US (though, weirdly, claimed by the village of Mumbles in South Wales as its own) in which a pocket is cut in a steak, stuffed with oysters and pinned closed before grilling.

crazed iconoclast, you could slip in a slice of raw onion, a couple of thinly sliced cornichons or, for all I know, generous slices of freshly foraged black truffle… though you would, of course, be dead to me if you did.

At this point, if you're feeling terribly cheffy, you could also store your sandwich, uncovered, in the fridge for a couple of hours. This dries the bread out and slightly increases its absorptive capacities – it is just a tweak, though… a refinement purely for the obsessed aficionado.

Now make up your egg wash. It's important that we refer to it as 'egg wash' because I'm convinced that it was regarding it as a 'batter' that got the Americans into this mess in the first place. Thoroughly beat a couple of large, fresh eggs with a little milk or cream. This is important for a complex chain of reasons:

1. If the sandwich is to be perfect, it must have a detectable taste of good egg…
2. and the texture must be cooked at the surface but a little soft and custardy underneath…
3. for this to happen you need the freshest eggs you can manage…
4. but fresh eggs aren't watery… the whites have an almost gel consistency…
5. thus, you need enough milk[20] or cream[21] to make the egg wash runny and easily absorbable…
6. but not so diluted that it won't set to the custardy consistency we need…
7. aargh… and don't forget to season it!

See? Complicated, huh?

Once you've made your egg wash you can dip in the sandwich. It is entirely impossible to suggest how long it might be allowed to soak as tastes vary, as will the absorbency of your bread, but you must persist. Make a Monte Cristo often and you will fine-tune your own technique.

There is only one thing we can all completely agree on as empirical, verifiable fact: the sandwich must now be fried slowly in ample butter.

[20] You can use skimmed or semi-skimmed if you wish…
[21] …ha ha! ONLY KIDDING!!!

Keep the temperature low enough initially that the butter doesn't scorch. This also extends the cooking time, giving the cheese time to melt and the ham time to donate its fatty benison to the surrounding bread.[22] Once the outside of the sandwich looks well set, any milk solids will have been absorbed, so the heat can be turned up to brown the sandwich without burning the butter.

The true beauty of this sandwich is that the soaked bread is as much the star as the filling. Once you get the hang of really letting it soak and timing the cooking to just set the egg, it has the texture of a sumptuously cheffy mousse or parfait.

They say that good things come in small packages, which is probably true, but better things come hot, in small packages sealed with egg and fried in butter.

OK. I think we've got this cracked. Our work here is done. Now we can hand it back to the Americans with happy hearts.

The Patty Melt

There are often terribly complicated origin myths for American diner sandwiches (see The French Dip on page 135) involving battles for the 'intellectual property' of a particular combination and tall tales about kitchen 'mistakes' that turn out to be blockbustingly popular with the punters. Almost anyone who's ever stood on a diner line and built a sandwich or flipped a burger will know these tales for the fabrications that they are. Most of the great 'inventions' spring automatically to hand from the standard diner *mise en place* when the cook is bored or has run out of something vital.

---

[22] Remember that little smear of butter we left inside the sandwich? It will melt and help the fats in the ham to run.

The patty melt is claimed to have been invented by Tiny Naylor, owner of a chain of eponymous diners in Los Angeles, at some point between 1930 and 1950. This may well be entirely true, but let me take you through the process and you can be the judge.

Imagine you're working in a diner, with all the regular accoutrements in front of you. Take one of the patties you use for a burger and lay it on the griddle to brown both sides quickly. Butter both sides of two slices of the rye bread you use for a Reuben. This will be what they call 'light rye'. A standard, packaged sandwich loaf that has just the faintest hint of brown fleck in it and an evanescent hint of caraway – the merest memory of Central Europe, a ghost of the *shtetl* but not enough to scare the horses. Lay the bread on the griddle, brown one side, then flip it. Top both slices with Swiss cheese (also from the Reuben ingredients), then place the patty on one slice and a handful of caramelised onions from the burger set-up on the other. Close up and finish as per a grilled cheese sandwich (see page 82).

That last bit is the key. Don't think you can get away with just building a cheeseburger with toasted bread instead of a bun. This is, as they say, 'a whole 'nother thing'. It's the way the cheese combines with the onions, melts into the bread and glues the lot together into a coherent mass that makes it a patty melt. Like a Philly cheesesteak but, if it's possible to comprehend, improved.

The thing is… it's bloody lovely. I don't know why everyone isn't eating patty melts all the time instead of poncey 'gourmet' burgers as big as your head. If Mr Naylor wants credit for this, he's more than welcome because this is a blessing to all humanity. All the loveliness of cheese, the crispy exterior of fried rye bread… it's almost *better* if your patty is a bit thin and undistinguished. Truth is… you can make a patty melt with a crummy pre-made burger and it will be *good*. You can even do the damned thing in a sandwich toaster. They say there are places where you can get a layer of Thousand Island dressing squirted in, but honestly, I think that might be too much for my tiny mind to comprehend. Can you imagine the joy?

The Great Sandwich Boom

A couple of decades ago, the Brits talked about sandwiches about as much as they do about their wages or their sex lives. A sandwich was something you did at home, in private. Sticking something like cheese, ham, Marmite or jam between two slices of bread was a serving suggestion and certainly not a culinary phenomenon.

If you wanted a sandwich for lunch you went to one of dozens of urban sandwich bars, usually Italian-owned, sometimes doubling as a greasy spoon breakfast joint, where you could choose your bread and your filling and watch the thing being made and wrapped in front of you.

Then, several key events happened in rapid succession. If you are so inclined, these can be read in a low voice, with dramatic background music in the manner of a true conspiracy theory:

> In the spring of 1980 Marks & Spencer begin selling the first pre-made sandwiches out of chilled display cabinets in their stores.

> In 1982 the milling company Molini Adriesi, in Verona, invent the ciabatta loaf.[23] Made with an extremely wet dough, it creates a light, soft-crust loaf that's the perfect size for a couple of single-serving sandwiches. It also toasts superbly.

> In 1985 Hans Blokmann, technical director of packaging supplier Danisco Flexible Otto Nielsen, invents an 'easy seal' package. Marks & Spencer begin using it immediately. In 1985 Marks & Spencer also begin baking ciabatta in the UK.

> In 1986 Pret A Manger begin their unstoppable rollout across the UK and, eventually, the world.[24]

[23] By 1999 it had been licensed to large bakeries in eleven countries. Soon afterwards it seems to have made a bid for freedom and now most bakeries produce at least one form of ciabatta.
[24] In 1984 the first Pret A Manger opened in Hampstead, London. The company went into liquidation after trading for eighteen months, whereupon the brand and visual assets were bought by Julian Metcalfe and Sinclair Beecham. The rest, as they say, is history.

Today the UK sandwich market is worth £6.25 billion (about $8 billion) per year, or 3.25 billion sandwiches[25] – that's the kind of interest and disposable income of which Ronald McDonald could only dream in his most fevered acquisitive fantasy. New sandwich shops should have sprung up everywhere offering a choice of fillings and a choice of breads, but instead our most convenient food has become a 'convenience food'.

Today very few shops make your sandwich in front of you or allow any degree of customisation. The chains assemble their sandwiches in their own kitchens and independent suppliers now take advantage of large production companies with a well-organised supply chain. Even the most remote petrol station or corner shop seems to sell a standard selection, delivered to them daily and probably made only, at worst, a day or two before. To keep them at optimum quality, most sandwiches are sold from temperature-controlled 'grab-'n'-go' units – not strictly refrigerators, but contraptions that ensure 'the product' stays within a safe 'temperature window' from the second it's made to the moment you open it to eat.[26]

It's hard to deny that people love sandwiches this way. They love the assured freshness, they love the guaranteed quality and consistency and they love the 'choice' they are offered of sometimes dozens of carefully researched flavours. One could argue that a cheery shop assistant, standing behind a counter packed with ingredients and asking you what you want in your bap, would give you all those benefits and more, but those businesses seem to have been drowned in a lumpy tide of 'crayfish and rocket in a lemon mayo'.

There is, though, one unexpected benefit to the mass sandwich industry and that is the panini. Yes, I know it should be a singular *'panino'*, but this is the odd thing – what we now call a 'panini' all over the world has very little to do with Italy and a lot to do with a particular combination of equipment and ingredients. For many years, Italian delis and sandwich shops had 'panini presses' in which any regular sandwich could be toasted. When the ciabatta arrived, it was found to be particularly good when toasted, but things got even better once commercial bakeries started offering their customers 'bake-off' bread.

---

[25] Figures from the British Sandwich & Food to Go Association.
[26] Only the grimmest joints, well off the delivery route, will need to offer 'gas-flushed' sandwiches, sealed in an inert atmosphere to give them a longer shelf life.

Bake-off bread is partially cooked, just to the point that it is fully risen and the crust has set, and then it's flash-frozen. The original idea was that shops and supermarkets could install a fan oven in which they could place the bake-off loaves, straight from the freezer, and offer their customers 'freshly baked' bread. It was a terrific idea and spawned a bread-based arms race amongst high-street shops to have the most delicious baking smells piped out of their doors as a kind of olfactory advertisement. (I interviewed a French chef who said that the defining experience of the UK was getting off the Eurostar and walking straight into the overpowering smell of bread.)

It didn't take sandwich sellers too long to discover another advantage of bake-off bread, though. You don't have to bother with the expensive fan oven. If you make up a sandwich with the half-baked loaf, you can finish it in a panini press whilst melting the filling. Soon the bakeries responded with purpose-made 'panini' bread – white, dense, in single-serving sizes and shaped a bit like a medium-sized espadrille but with a marginally less pronounced flavour profile. The perfect vehicle.

Of course, you can't have lettuce, or arguably even tomato, in your 'panini' – but you can make them up by the dozen and hold them in the fridge. Any half-skilled member of staff can whip them out and slap them into the jaws of the panini press and the result is… well, it's really quite good. Sure, it bears the same relationship to a gorgeously crafted toasted sandwich as baked beans do to a *cassoulet*… but we're talking about snack foods here and, as we've established, baked beans are damn good in context.

It's actually possible to buy reasonable bake-off baguettes in a supermarket. I think they're designed as emergency standbys for the kind of people who fear they might have to whip up a dinner party for six at half an hour's notice. They are made by large commercial bakeries but, as is surprisingly possible with this technique, without needing many additives. Actually, freezing half-cooked bread can work extraordinarily well… if you've eaten warm sourdough or freshly baked rolls in a quality restaurant in the last few years, you've almost certainly been eating bread that was custom-made off-site and frozen for 'baking off' later on.

You'll need lots of butter in your sandwich – you want it to melt into the bread – or you could use olive oil. Cheese is a structurally vital part of a panini, so you'll need something that has good melting qualities and, perhaps, a bit of stringiness. I usually grate a mix of cheeses with a base of the solid 'pizza-style' mozzarella for texture, then something rich to give it body, maybe a Comté, Gruyère, some fontina or even a punchy Cheddar, depending on the ethnicity of my remaining ingredients. Then you'll need some superb charcuterie – one of those German smoked hams, a finely sliced chorizo, maybe even a smear of 'nduja.

To get the proper corner-shop effect, it's important to apply pressure to the lid of your panini press at the point when the fats in the cheese and the meat begin to melt. Squeeze until the juices run, then release the pressure and the doughy bread soaks them up like a sponge. You can serve the panini with a salad on the side or some sort of healthy salsa for dipping, but there's no practical way to get attractive leaves or healthy vegetation into a panini – but then, that's not the point. It doesn't really need anything else. This is entirely an exercise in balancing cheese and charcuterie, in getting the right degree of 'soak' into the bread and finishing the exterior crust to perfection in your sandwich grill.

The Love That Dare Not Speak Its Name

I'm not going to patronise you by mansplaining mayonnaise. You know how it's made, you know the tricks and hints, yours is probably better than mine and we both know that Hellmann's is pretty damn good at a pinch. We know the importance of mayonnaise, as a binding agent in fillings and as a lubricant to greedy throats. It has been suggested, and only half in jest, that Pret A Manger isn't actually a sandwich shop but a front for a mayonnaise empire, so promiscuous are they in its application. But we forget too easily that, before they opened their doors to a desperate public, mayonnaise was something extra you had to ask for. If you went into a British sandwich shop, your bread would be buttered – or in extreme cases, margarined – the filling would go on and, if you were feeling a bit adventurous, you asked for the lettuce leaf and slice of tomato that were quietly expiring under the sweaty glass counter. You had to ask for mayo and someone went and fetched the jar, uttering epithets ('Where does 'e think 'e is… Fifth bleedin' Avenue?'). We have a lot to thank Pret for… but we'd do well to remember that, BP (the era Before Pret), there was an alternative to mayonnaise. We also had (why do I feel I have to whisper this?) salad cream.

It must have been around the 1980s that salad cream – invariably Heinz – began to disappear from our diet, supplanted by the more fashionable and cosmopolitan mayo. It is fair to say that it was sweet, it was vinegary and it was perhaps a less sophisticated taste, but what is unforgivable is that salad cream was driven off by class pretensions. It was one of those products characterised as 'naff' by a generation of food writers and was metaphorically forced out of town by a howling mob with pitchforks. Which is a shame because salad cream is (again, whisper it) really nice.

Fresh mayonnaise is one of Escoffier's mother sauces – a complicated emulsion that takes a cheffy hand to create and with a subtle taste. It's there to provide a smooth texture, to lend richness, but, of its very nature, it's not supposed to intrude on the delicate flavours of the food over which it's carefully drizzled. It's basically an egg yolk as an emulsive base for as much 'good' oil as you can coax it to take, with a touch of vinegar to cut back the richness and a hint of mustard. It is not a robust thing. And it was never the right thing for the classic English salad. Salad cream, on the other hand, is an inversion of very similar ingredients. Start with a hard-boiled egg yolk, rubbed through a sieve, and a generous dollop of English mustard, ferociously sharp and yellow with turmeric. Begin by beating in a bland oil – rapeseed is great – until you start to get a mayo-like thickening (a *lot* easier with the hard-boiled yolk), then add a similar amount of double cream. Damn right! Double cream. Talk about richness. Season with lemon juice, white pepper and salt.

Away from the bottle (which, as I remember it, always had a kind of collar or pie frill of rubbery, dry, old sauce just below the cap), salad cream is a game-changing addition to your sandwich 'practice', a yin to mayo's yang and a blessing on humanity. Make a batch and try it anywhere that mayo is mentioned in a recipe. Its more pronounced flavours will wake up your ingredients where mayo simply evens them out into homogeneity.[27]

[27] Particularly try it as the base for prawn cocktail sauce. The standard 'Marie Rose' served in England is still a depressingly sweet 'ketchunaise'. Proper salad cream is awesome on its own as a seafood dressing or tinted pink with a little tomato purée that's been cooked in a dry pan to remove its rather nasty acidity. It will transform your life. You may thank me later.

Ou Sont Les Tuna Salades D'Antan?

I spent years in pursuit of the perfect tuna salad. Years wasted simply because, as it turned out, I was facing in the wrong direction. The best tuna sandwiches I remembered were in a particular diner in San Francisco where the counterman would take the stuff out of a stainless-steel tub with a big ice-cream scoop. He'd dollop two perfect hemispheres of it onto a slice of brown bread, leer every time, at some internal Benny Hill sight gag, and then smush the top down with a second slice.

The bread had to be American brown sliced. An entirely weird product that had some of the cues of British brown bread – a vague tan and chippings of bran – but was also definitely and emphatically sweet. I'd suggest molasses, but it was probably nothing so natural.

The idea should have been simple: mayo and tinned tuna with a few minor embellishments. And so I set out to replicate it. I started with decent tinned tuna steak in brine and a properly made mayonnaise, and it tasted of nothing. I started upping the seasonings, adding grated onion, garlic powder, Old Bay Seasoning… all the usual suspects of the diner's store cupboard, but nothing would wake it up. I added lemon juice, which was revolting. Fruit and fish? Was I mad?

I began to cut back the mayo. Surely by reducing the bland condiment I could make it taste of something?

I'm not saying I suffered any kind of crisis of faith here. I didn't sit in the corner of the kitchen weeping like a fallen priest… but this took place over several years and it was a bloody long time to waste chasing a sandwich. Eventually I remembered something. At a place I'd worked in in another part of the States – OK, I'll come clean, I was covering shifts in a small correctional facility – the 'chef' had made the tuna salad in an industrial kitchen mixer. What if… what if I was heading the wrong way?

I bought a very large cheap can of tuna chunks. Still sustainably sourced (I'm not a barbarian), but a cheaper cut of less-pretty meat. Most importantly, this was the oily stuff. Oily and strong-tasting, plus it was poached and packed in oil. I confess it reminded me a little of cat food as

I poured it into the mixer bowl and turned on the paddle, but if we were going back to first principles, this was the way to start. The meat broke up quickly and began to combine with its own oil, so I began to pour in the mayo. Reader, it drank the stuff like a man in a desert. I just kept pouring and it kept absorbing. This was how Joël Robuchon must have felt the day he realised that he could get more butter than potato into a serving of mashed potato. Even unseasoned, a spoonful drew Proustian tears.

I don't use the mixer any more. A big can of tuna will drink a dustbin full of mayonnaise and even I can't shift that much, but it reversed my approach to tuna mayo altogether. Don't go 'premium' on the fish – you need strong flavour. Keep your 'ventresca' for your *salade Niçoise*. But, above all, understand that this is about a great deal of mayonnaise. Today, recalibrated and centred on firm foundations, I can tweak and build with abandon. I like some sharp little nonpareil capers mixed in. Chopped spring onion is no bad thing. I can get all arty with Espelette pepper in a knowing tip-of-the-beret to the Côte d'Azur; minced, pickled pimientos for colour, finely chopped celery for texture and crunch. Last week, I even chopped in hard-boiled egg, and it was still a thousand miles ahead, in a direct line, from the tuna salad *du temps perdu*.

The Tuna Melt

There are many reasons to love Heston Blumenthal – not least, the kind of enthusiastic forensic nerdery that made him deconstruct the simple hamburger in *In Search of Perfection* – but even he went too far, I would argue, in attempting to recreate sheets of yellow 'burger cheese'. Burger cheese, sometimes known as 'American cheese', is regulated by the FDA under US Code of Federal Regulations Title 21 (Food and Drugs), Part 133 (Cheeses and Related Cheese Products). It can contain a blend of cheeses (solid or powdered), cream, milk fat, water, salt, artificial colour, oils and spices that is emulsified, set into sheets and individually packaged. This can be called 'pasteurised processed cheese' if it contains more than

51 per cent cheese products by weight. If less is present, it's labelled 'pasteurised processed cheese *food*' and, let's be honest, it's still bloody gorgeous.

Heston judiciously combined premium cheeses with a chemical widely available in pharmacies as a treatment for cystitis[28] to create a cheesy sheet that melted properly, but the question every burger lover screamed at the screen was: 'WHY?'

We know that ketchup is a noxious mix of sugar syrup, colouring, MSG and vegetable extracts, yet we do not mess with it. Further, almost all chefs acknowledge gladly that only one brand of tommy K matters in spite of its industrialised manufacture and uninspiring ingredients. It is a *sui generis* condiment and as such is respected and left alone.

I shall not rest until burger cheese is afforded the same honour. It is a barbarous, manufactured commodity with no redeeming features, dietary or aesthetic. It is also a perfect condiment, in no need of improvement and not to be deconstructed... it just happens to come shrink-wrapped in plastic and set in rubbery sheets. Just regard it as such and use it as freely and without guilt as you would tomato ketchup.

Which brings us, inexorably, to the tuna melt... a sandwich so weird that most Brits refuse to believe it actually exists. A sandwich that has to be explained and, even then, provokes incredulity, fear and loathing.

To begin with, the tuna melt involves fish and cheese, which, in pretty much any cuisine anywhere in the world, is a complete non-starter. And yet somehow it survives... nay, thrives.

To make a tuna melt you'll need some truly awful brown sandwich bread. Nothing with any proper nutritional value. You could, if you were aiming to be clever, go for something artisanal, but be aware that the slight sweet maltiness of the packaged stuff is key here. If you go for something virtuous, make sure it has some kind of molasses content.

---

[28] The jury is still out on how he made this particular discovery.

You can use the tuna salad discussed previously as filling, but the really savage amounts of mayo make things a little indigestible. Though a diner would just slop on the standard tuna salad mix, I'd counsel something lighter on the mayo and stretched with a little vegetable matter. Celery is vital. Certainly some finely minced onion and maybe some sweetish red pepper for colour and general virtuousness. Some add a splash of vinegar to sharpen things up, still others chop a gherkin finely and run it through, which has a similar effect. Dammit, it's so healthy it's almost a salad.

Put the bread slices through a toaster first, then mound one slice with the tuna mixture and smear the other liberally with mayo. Now it's time to add the cheese. Most diners will offer a choice of cheese on a burger: 'American', the odd yellow stuff we've already discussed, and 'Swiss'. This is not, as one might hope, a fine, cave-aged Emmental, but 'American Swiss', which is a rindless, pasteurised and processed cheese, sweeter than the standard yellow wax and sometimes graced with one or two decorative holes. It will never have been near Switzerland and nobody has dared to ask the Swiss how they feel about it.

You can choose freely what you're going to top your melt with, at least between these two options, but it's important that you don't drift off-piste and use anything like a 'proper' cheese. Because here is the most important thing to remember… fish and cheese really don't go together, and a tuna melt only works because *tinned tuna doesn't taste much like fish and processed cheese doesn't taste much like cheese*. This is the key to truly understanding the tuna melt.

Drape your chosen 'cheese' over your mound of 'fish' and place both pieces of toast under a grill. The cheese will melt – don't allow it to brown or even much more than bubble – and the top piece will 'fry' a little as the oil in the mayo heats up. Put on the lid and serve.

The truth is, it's rather lovely. Once you realise that it's not really supposed to taste too much of either of its constituent ingredients, you're safe to enjoy one of the greatest and most misunderstood comfort foods.

Egg Mayonnaise

Another deceptively simple, classic sandwich filling is what the Brits call egg mayonnaise and the Americans call egg salad. It is, of course, easy to smash up a couple of hard-boiled eggs in a squirt of shop-bought mayo, but that is to miss the infinite subtleties of one of the finest and most luxurious things you can place between slices of bread. Bear with me here. Not the homogenous eggy slurry they pipe into the sarnies at your local corner shop, jam into triangular cardboard boxes and then stick on the shelf at the far end, just so those people who come in every single lunchtime but still can't pluck up enough courage to experiment will find something utterly, utterly bland enough to suit their pusillanimous lack of moral or sensual fibre. That stuff is miserable.

I am talking about the real deal. At the estimable St. John restaurant, where chef Fergus Henderson effectively established the rules for proper eating, one of the most popular lunchtime snacks is an egg mayonnaise sandwich, made with their own sourdough bread, spankingly fresh free-range eggs and homemade mayo. If you know the routine, you can take your sandwich up to the bar, where a modest tip to the barman will produce a couple of cured anchovies. The barman lifts the lid of your sandwich and drapes the fish over the mound of egg and something entirely magical happens.

As mayonnaise is made of egg and oil, you could argue that putting it on an egg is like putting ketchup on a tomato, but this would be to miss the point. Good egg mayonnaise is about the eggs expressing their egginess. I don't mean in a comedy, fart gag, stink bomb way. I mean the kind of voluptuous richness of a fine custard, a perfectly executed omelette or hollandaise.

You need to start with excellent hard-boiled eggs, which, in itself, used to be a problem. For many years, with eggs being of varying sizes and methods for cooking varying wildly, the general wisdom was to boil the things for ages… well, at least ten minutes… and then let them cool. This indeed produced an egg with a hard yolk, but the yolk was usually covered with a layer of depressing grey and the whites the texture of long-boiled squid. Different chefs swore by different methods, but there was little science.

It could surely not be beyond the wit of man to create an algorithm that took into account the starting temperature of the egg, its circumference and, therefore, the ideal time in which it needs to be immersed in boiling water. Actually, the maths turned out to be so easy that several bright young people created apps for mobile phones into which you can enter the data and set a timer. I favour an app called Egg Master, which, last time I looked, was entirely gratis and has resulted in several years of successful egg mastery on my part.

Today we can be much more selective about the textures in our egg mayo and true greatness is within our grasp. In a traditional egg mayo, the dry yolk would absorb great quantities of mayo. Now we can plan to leave the yolks just short of completely solid so that they create moisture themselves and reduce the amount of mayo needed.[29] It's subtle, but it shifts the balance of flavour from the mayo to the egg.

I take four free-range eggs that I know to be good and fresh and measure their diameters using the app. They haven't been kept in the fridge, so I can assume that their current temperature, from shell to core, is the ambient temperature of the kitchen, which I measure with a thermometer and enter into the app, too. The app tells me I need to cook the eggs for six minutes and thirty-seven seconds, so I lower them into boiling water and set the timer running. As the alert pings, I run the eggs under cold water to immediately stop them cooking.

Next I make up an egg's worth of mayonnaise. Personally, I like it with lashings of mustard and quite a pronounced lemon flavour so that it really is pretty indistinguishable from the salad cream we talked about before. You can, of course, use a decent shop-bought mayo or even regular bottled salad cream. Add the mayo (or salad cream) to the eggs a little at a time, mashing them roughly with a fork. Don't overdo this. You need to see serious chunks of white and one or two noticeable chunks of undisturbed yellow yolk. For me, this is enough, once salt and pepper have been adjusted, but American recipes often add finely minced celery, paprika or even grainy mustard. They may have a point.

---

[29] We now know that the temperature at which a yolk will set to an ideal degree of 'fudginesss' is 73.9°C (165°F).

I think egg mayo works best on a really rustic sourdough, chewy of crust and with enough sourness to scare off amateurs. This is solely a personal thing and it relies on the egg mayo being anything but bland. Have faith that the egginess of your ingredients will carry through and don't fall back on bland bread.

The Tamago Sando – Japanese Egg Mayo

Kewpie is a Japanese brand of mayonnaise, different enough from our own to be instantly better in many dishes. Even the highest-quality pre-made mayos in the west contain quite a quantity of water along with whole eggs, distilled vinegar and sugar. The idea is that the condiment should supply a pleasant mouthfeel, with the individual flavours so well balanced that there's nothing polarising in any particular direction. The whole point of a thick smear of Hellmann's is that it enhances what it's served with, so if you eat a spoonful by itself, you'll be unlikely to distinguish egginess, much vinegar or any trace of mustard.

Kewpie is also made with soya bean oil, and it uses only the yolks of the eggs, along with rice vinegar, which is a little sweeter than distilled, no extra water and some MSG. Some people feel that Kewpie is more like salad cream than mayonnaise – not, as we have already established, a problem for me. I personally find that Kewpie tastes more like a fresh mayonnaise that I'd make to my own taste… more egg, vinegar and mustard.

It's the Kewpie that distinguishes the *tamago sando* – the cult egg mayo sandwich found in *konbini* [30] across Japan.

Shops like 7-Eleven, Lawson and FamilyMart stock all kinds of pre-made snack food, but the *tamago sando* is served in all of them, without exception. It has, somehow, become as defining a sandwich of the Japanese takeaway world as the cheese and ham is to our own.

[30] A loan word from English meaning 'convenience store'.

Like any *sando*, the *tamago* requires *shokupan* bread – white, light and largely without redeeming features. The eggs are cooked carefully to be just the tiniest bit short of fully set and then blitzed almost to death with lots of Kewpie mayo and a little *sanshō* pepper. The egg salad component is almost a smooth paste, with perhaps just the smallest hints of cubed white providing texture, but the finishing touch is a halved egg placed in the middle of each *sando*, buried in the egg salad. It may have something to do with its success that a *tamago sando* looks so completely adorable when cut across (and Instagrammed…), or it may be that the hyper-eggy Kewpie mayo, with all the component flavours singing out, can do the impossible and improve on the perfection of the Western egg mayo sarnie.

The BLT

Some classic sandwiches are a clean canvas for cheffy creativity. It's rare, these days, to find a club sandwich that doesn't have a 'twist'. Sometimes it's avocado, sometimes a flavoured mayo or a grating of some interesting cheese; occasionally it will be an artisanal bread, 'curated' by the chef to enhance locally sourced ingredients; some feature fried chicken, house-cured bacon… and one or two of them are actually pleasant. But nobody – thanks be to whichever gods oversee the kitchen – messes with the BLT.

It's possible that this is because of the name. 'Bacon, lettuce and tomato' is fairly prescriptive. Any supernumerary major ingredient messes with the billing. 'Chef Nigel's bacon, lettuce and tomato with cheese' doesn't work. It's marvellously self-limiting. But there's another reason. Put simply, the BLT – precisely as it stands – is the perfect sandwich.

I don't use the word 'perfect' lightly. It should never really appear in a book of recipes because, in the normal run of things, it's just not possible to give written instructions for something that's full of an impossible number of variables and is, ultimately, entirely a matter of personal taste. There is no 'perfect beef stew', because my perfect is not your perfect and there's no way we can make it the same on any two occasions anyway.

The BLT is something different, though. Its origin, history and the unique combination of ingredients mean it constitutes a kind of ideal. The BLT persists in its pure form because, in principle, it is as close to perfect as a sandwich can be, even if our executions may fall short on occasion.

The bacon, lettuce and tomato sandwich begins life in the American diner some time after 1900. There are one or two recipe books that suggest sandwiches a bit like it, but the purest form isn't mentioned. It's perhaps too simple and obvious to please a publisher. But to anyone who's ever worked the counter at a diner, it's entirely obvious how the sandwich came into being. As we saw with the invention of the patty melt, everything on the diner menu has evolved from the restrictive combination of the equipment (the griddle or hotplate) and the *mise en place* (the range of cheap ingredients that the cook sets up at the grill station at the beginning of each shift).

If a hungry driver walked into any diner across the US from 1900 onwards and asked, 'Can you make me a sandwich?', the grill monkey would reach for the sliced bread, grab a few rashers of the bacon left over from breakfast, take some tomato and lettuce from the garnish pots and finish it all with a flourish of mayo. The fastest combination. The cheapest ingredients. Nobody 'invented' it any more than they could patent the idea of sitting around a fire, banging out a rhythm and dancing. It just happens from the stuff that's there. This is the root of the BLT. A kind of form-follows-function, pared-to-the-bone 'rightness' that underpins everything.

Because the BLT is a diner staple all over the US, it has one other phenomenal advantage. It has been served, consistently, to the most powerful and effective focus group in food history. Diners are democratic dining institutions, largely untroubled by class distinction and populated by hungry people who want decent food fast and affordably. The cooks buy ingredients regularly, cook to order and respond instantly to customer feedback. The best consultants in the world could not come up with a better, broader and more robust system of product development. For over a hundred years this sandwich has stayed, in every real sense, the same. People have, in their millions, made the choice to return to it – chefs have tried variations but returned to it, owners have probably tried to cut corners but always... always returned to the one, pure, true way.

Nobody knows who first called it a 'BLT', but it's classic diner slang. It needs the life experience of a forty-five-year-old career waitress called Blanche, living in a trailer on the edge of town, who's been on her feet for a double shift, to further reduce the simplest idea to a barked acronym. Dictionaries record the first uses of 'BLT' in the 1970s, but it must have already been in common use over a thousand strips of battered melamine in a thousand small burgs for decades.

Like any good meal, a classic sandwich must be balanced, and the thing about a BLT is that it's almost impossible to mess up the balance. Bacon is the key protein here, but it would be wrong to think of this as a garnished bacon sandwich. The combination – which, incidentally, is foolproof – is everything.

The bacon shouldn't be anything special. Diner bacon would be chosen for the most cost-effective combination of medium-sliced, medium-smoked, enough fat for the fat lovers, enough meat for the fat-avoiders. You could, if you chose, favour back or streaky, smoked or unsmoked, but you'd be closer to the original if you had a mix of everything.

The tomato is as vital to the mix as the bacon. In a diner, they'll choose big, flat-ended tomatoes so that they get the maximum number of slices, preferably big enough to be used singly, thus cutting down on faffing during assembly. A diner owner would really like tomatoes to be foot-long cylinders because they hate throwing away the ends. We, on the other hand, are sophisticated enough to know that they should combine sweet, sharp and cold in order to counterpoint the hot, salt and fat of the bacon.

The iceberg lettuce might well be the most reviled vegetable in history. Admittedly it has little flavour, but there are plenty of other vegetables that don't blow your head off, so why do chefs and food writers tap so deep into their bile reserves for this innocuous ingredient?

It's probably something to do with its history. There are all sorts of stories about the origin of 'crisphead' or iceberg lettuce… from the suggestion that it was developed at the turn of the twentieth century by growers in the north-west of the US to be more resistant to the cold and have a longer growing season, to the story that they were the first lettuces robust enough to be packed in ice and shipped from California all across

the United States.[31] It's certainly true that they have a tremendous shelf life, both in the shop and at home in the fridge, that they have few nutrients in their anaemic leaves and that in the 1970s they became demonised in battles over the working conditions of immigrant field workers in California (still the largest producer of lettuce outside of China).

Iceberg, with its highly commercial history and technologically advanced supply chain, is as far from the ideal of gathering a few simple leaves with a trug in the garden and tossing them in a light dressing as it's possible to imagine. Iceberg was the first 'salad' many ordinary urban Americans ever saw and then it was likely to be hewn into quarters and coated in some terrifying proprietary dressing… which may go a little way towards explaining why American food icon Craig Claiborne started an effective personal crusade against it or why Alice Waters declared it 'plebeian'.

The problem, of course, is that iceberg is great. Blue cheese dressing needs a structural framework, a Big Mac needs a layer that at least attempts to look green, something's got to support the prawns in a cocktail… these are all the noblest of duties in the eyes of any but the most doctrinaire food elitists. And the most glorious and perfect use to which iceberg can be put is as the 'L' in the BLT.

A leafy cos or butterhead lettuce would be overwhelmed. A frisée might intrigue, but it would be too bitter and would pull messily out of the sandwich instead of yielding to the bite. Romaine is leathery, Little Gem too sweet or too assertive in its lettuciness.

Iceberg, chilled from the fridge, is the foil to the hot, fatty bacon – it resists its influence, refusing to wilt – and support to the mayo. Weirdly, iceberg is the only part of the BLT that admits to variation. You can shred it, apply it as separated leaves or slice the whole damn head across into thin 'lettuce steaks'. *Of course* it hasn't got as many nutrients as a handful of baby spinach, mesclun or kale… but really, if you need to go to your bacon sandwich for vitamins, you're already way beyond help and should probably be incarcerated in a spa somewhere having orange juice and cod liver oil shot up your bottom hourly.

---

[31] Palpably untrue. They would brown and rot in contact with ice.

Now to the key element of the sandwich: the bread. It must be white because all the delicious nut, caramel and malt notes of a brown or wholemeal loaf would be entirely wasted or would confuse the purity of the main tastes. It must be machine-sliced to be in correct proportion to the filling – yes, I know a sourdough doorstep looks terrific on Instagram, but unless you can unhinge your lower jaw like an anaconda or you've been gifted by the food gods with a flip-top head, it's going to make 'getting the sandwich into your mouth' the main focus of your eating experience rather than 'enjoying it'.

The bread must be toasted – this has always been the way. It may, originally, have been a way of using up bread that was just past fresh, or to ensure that the bread didn't get soggy, soaking up mayo and tomato leakings while it sat on the pass waiting for the waiter to pick it up. You could declare that the toasting adds a certain Maillard caramelisation to the bread, but I've never been able to detect it. More important is the fact that the lovely bronzed colour that cheap sliced gets in the toaster is at least partially a product of its higher sugar content. Crappy sliced white is quite sweet, which balances the salty bacon as if calibrated on a vernier scale.

Assembly isn't complicated, but certain rules must be followed. Combined in the wrong way, the ingredients of a BLT can be soggy, limp and unfulfilling, so building the sandwich is about combining the hot and cold elements – straight from the pan or fridge – so that they maintain separation and balance. Fat, salt, sweet and blandness must blend while the whole construction crunches in all the places it can crunch.

Fry the bacon while lightly toasting the bread, then put it to one side. Quickly flash one side of each toasted slice through the hot fat left in the pan. This adds to the flavour and also goes a little way towards making the slice waterproof and resistant to sogging. As soon as it's out of the pan, slather the fried side of each slice with mayonnaise. Use a knife if you wish, but as you should be using the ready-made stuff, it's easier to just pipe it on from a squeezy bottle. Making your own mayo would be beyond pointless.

Lay down the bacon first, then ample tomato and the iceberg. This order is vital, as it keeps the tomato, the main source of dampness, away from the toast. Nail the sandwich shut with cocktail sticks – holding it together in such a way that you don't need to smush the top down with your hand.

By doing this, the ingredients retain lightness and separation, they look great and they're not forced into combination until the diner is ready to pick it up and squeeze it into his or her mouth.

Slice the sandwich across diagonally once – a BLT comes as two halves, only clubs come in quarters – and serve opened to show the cut face. Do not serve with chips; a BLT is a self-contained meal. For similar reasons, do not attempt to add superfluous salad as a 'garnish', or even a pickle. You can, if you're just desperate to mess with perfection, throw down a handful of crisps, but it's hard to see why you'd feel the need.

The Room Service Club

There are some phrases in the food world that carry an emotional import that's out of kilter with their simple meaning. 'A bowl of soup' carries no more semiotic load than you'd imagine at first sight – it's a bowl with soup in it – but say '*pot-au-feu*' to a Frenchman or 'full fry-up' to a Brit and you evoke a complex structure of beliefs, feelings and loyalties.

There is one term, though, for which I suspect the effect is international. Could there be two more evocative words than 'room service'?

I'm sure you, dear reader, are a jet-setting habitué of the world's finest hotels and so for you the memory may be lost in a haze of luxury, but I remember with astonishing clarity the first time I ordered room service.

My sister was PA to an Australian TV executive and a team of them were staying at the George V in Paris on some kind of terrifyingly important sales drive. Somebody had left a vital tape in the London office, so little Sis called. 'Grab your passport, pick up the tape and deliver it to the hotel this evening. I'll arrange a room for you *but stay in it*. Order room service. Be gone in the morning.' To be clear, there was nothing in the delivery transaction itself that required such cloak and daggery; it was simply that, at that point, I'd just escaped a provincial art college, was living in a truly repugnant Peckham squat and looked, not to put too fine a point on it, like a roadie who'd been fired for poor personal hygiene.

Room service was a split of champagne and a club sandwich and was, predictably, sublime. But through the long years and numberless hotels (of varying quality) since that first experience, I've realised that the appeal of room service is not actually about the excellence of what's served.

Chefs hate doing room service. Some of the best restaurants in the world are located in grand hotels and kitchen facilities are often shared. Cooks are never overjoyed to be pulled from prepping a three-star dish in order to knock up the sort of Scooby Snack you might assemble while drunk and serve it with a side of fries. Punters, on the other hand, couldn't be more delighted by the idea of kicking off their shoes amidst all the froth and frippery, cranking up some dreck on cable TV and lying in bed eating something that is guaranteed to be 100 per cent delicious and unchallenging.

Chefs know – and loathe the fact – that you can't mess with the room service classics. Substituting a homemade mayo for Hellmann's might give you a chance to shine in front of your boss, but lemon mayo, pesto, toasted brioche, avocado, sumac or any one of a million possible 'twists' or 'takes' on the chef's behalf will result in the thing being left outside the door, untouched under its crumpled napkin.

If you travel a lot, room service becomes a touchstone almost as important as home cooking. It's easy to feel lonely and deracinated in a hotel room, a deep anomie induced by the rigidly corporate surroundings. In such an environment, tiny personal rituals become vital. Room service can be elevated to an almost religious rite by waking up late with no meetings to attend and a medium–severe-grade hangover. At this point, the peace – the feeling of being completely self-contained while a frenzied world runs mad around you – approaches the monastic.

I'm not entirely sure a club sandwich actually works without room service. I suppose it might be appropriate on a terrace by the side of the pool, perhaps as a snack in the bar, but it seems intrinsically bound up in hotel-style service.

I suppose if you did follow the BLT method but included an extra layer of toasted bread and some sliced poached chicken breast you'd have a facsimile, but you'd just know there was something amiss. It's not just that a BLT is cut into triangular halves and a club into quarters, it's everything that this preparation implies – the hassled counterman, halving one with a single stroke of the knife, the commis chef titivating the other onto a plate, garnishing it and covering it with a cloche to be rushed to your room.

The Fish Finger Sandwich

If you ever find yourself at a loose end, light the fire, pour yourself a glass of something and curl up with a copy of the EU standards for '7.5kg fish blocks'. I'll grant you it might not be as compelling as *The Old Man and the Sea*, but it's a darned sight more relevant to our consumption of fish.

Most fish these days are processed at sea within minutes of being caught. They are gutted, filleted, sometimes skinned and, if they can be sold to a restaurant or fishmonger who's keen to make a spectacular display, the fillets will be frozen individually and intact. But for most of our fish needs – the breaded Filets-O-Fish, goujons and princely fish fingers – there is a different process. The boneless fish flesh is packed into a mould or 'frame' and frozen into a block measuring 482 x 254 x 62.7mm (19 x 10 x 2½ inches) with a standard weight of 7.5 kg (or about 16½ lb).[32]

There are different grades of fish block available. Top-notch ones will contain whole fillets of a single species of fish. These can sometimes contain 'voids' where the fillets don't pack precisely, so the process of packing can be more expensive and labour-intensive. Easier to create are the slightly lower-grade blocks in which smaller pieces of fish are used up. Simplest of all, and cheapest, are blocks made of minced fish where the size of the piece doesn't matter and different species of white fish can be mixed.[33]

[32] Block tolerance +/- 1.0mm.
[33] Meat pieces are processed the same way in industrial butchery. It was standard blocks of frozen 'beef' pieces that turned out to be the eventual cause of the Europe-wide horse meat scandal in 2013.

Fish fingers are made by sawing the blocks into pieces and coating them in breadcrumbs – so you can see that a good-quality, expensive one means you're getting a large piece of cod or haddock, perfectly preserved, seconds from the sea. You can certainly argue that mixing the catch and avoiding waste of smaller or less-attractive bits of fish can make fish fingers terrifically sustainable. You can also appreciate how some 'commodity' fish fingers can be so frighteningly cheap.

Fish fingers were invented by the prolific American inventor and entrepreneur Clarence Birdseye and were first trialled in the UK in 1955. There was a huge market for cheap and easy protein during Britain's post-war austerity and Birdseye ran trials in Southampton and South Wales on frozen, ready-to-cook herring sticks. Herring was plentiful and extremely nourishing, but the researchers had failed to take into account British squeamishness around the smell of cooking fish. Customers, they were surprised to discover, turned up their noses at the herring sticks, but they loved the control product in the test… a stick made entirely of bland cod.

Today, for better or worse, the cod fish finger is seen to represent the British diet: loved for its convenience, its ease of cooking, its unchallenging flavour and the fact that it can be cooked almost entirely without smell. Neighbours with more advanced food cultures and a healthier relationship with fish stand frankly bewildered… and yet…

There is something indefinable, something innately glorious about a fish finger sandwich that simultaneously subverts the humble origins of the fish stick and raises two fingers to haters in the wider world of gastronomy. And what elevates the fish finger sandwich to glory is the sauce.

You can, of course, make your sarnie with mayonnaise or some kind of pre-made tartare sauce, and that would just be extraordinarily delicious. But what we need here is something that takes the blandness of the finger and the soft, smooth canvas of the thick-sliced white bread, and paints upon it a complex and profoundly moving masterpiece. Something creamy, rich, spiked with acidic notes, fragrant with herbs and fulfilling enough in texture to be a dish on its own. What we need is a *gribiche*-y tartare!

Tartare is a sauce specifically recommended for fish. It's made on a base of mayo with the addition of vinegar for sharpness, chopped capers for sourness and tarragon for additional flavour. You're also quite likely to find it in a plastic pouch in your chip shop. *Gribiche*, on the other hand, is a nobler and more complicated thing. It's traditionally been applied to cold meats and perhaps for that reason it caught on in British cuisine far more firmly than, for example, its cousin, *rémoulade*.

Start with four hard-boiled eggs and remove the yolks of three of them. Rub the yolks through a sieve and then make them back into a paste with a tablespoon or so of Dijon mustard. Now you can start stirring in olive oil the way you would with a mayonnaise and, indeed, you'll soon see it begin to emulsify and build volume, becoming glossy and smooth. I'd usually keep going until about 250ml (9fl oz) of oil has been sucked up. If your olive oil is particularly aristocratic stuff, you can always substitute something like rapeseed oil instead, or even some crème fraîche for half of it.

Now you have your base, which will somewhat resemble the salad cream described on page 95. Now it's time to transform it. Start with a handful of finely minced capers and cornichons. Vary the proportion as you see fit, but be aware that the cornichons contain a fair amount of liquid and are pretty vinegary… adjust the rest of your seasoning accordingly. Add finely chopped tarragon (and chervil if you can find it). Finally, break up the remaining egg and egg whites with a fork into rough chunks, stir them into the mixture and adjust the seasoning once more.

This will produce a substantial bowl of *gribiche* – far more than you need for the sandwich, but you will find that, if it's half as good as it should be, the adjustment phase will go on for quite a while and you'll be doing it with a large spoon. I've yet to find a restaurant where *gribiche* is served as a starter with a couple of bits of sourdough toast, but it's only a matter of time.

Some people would add just an evanescent wraith of fishiness to the gribiche with an anchovy or two crushed in at the beginning. It's a brilliant, indeed a defining touch. But we know of something better, don't we? Something delicious, just mildly fishy and supplied in a convenient, breaded finger shape.

Butter a couple of slices of soft white sandwich loaf. I wouldn't go for the pre-sliced stuff… things are going to get messy here, so you need thick

slices of something with dimensional stability and strength in the face of wetness. Smear a thin layer of *gribiche*-y tartare on the bottom slice, then lay on enough fish fingers to plank it right across. I know some people cut the fingers in half laterally, but I honestly feel they just lack courage in their convictions and should probably consult a qualified counsellor or perhaps a priest. Now spoon on a really very substantial layer of the (inadequate word) 'sauce'. A pile, in fact. A small mound. The sort of size you could bury a Viking king in… with all his retainers and his plunder… and his boat. Then perch the second slice on top. If you get this bit right, you should be looking at a side elevation like a VW Beetle with a mattress on the roof rack. Cut in half very carefully, serve with due ceremony and eat over the sink.

The Katsu Doorstep

The fish finger sandwich might be resolutely British, but it has a singularly exotic cousin in the *katsu sando*, a Japanese street-food sandwich of similar vintage to the fish finger, which has recently gained international recognition and fashionably cult status.

As often happens with incoming cultural phenomena, the name originates outside the Japanese language and has been cheerily adopted. '*Katsu*' is short for *katsuretsu*, meaning 'cutlet', and *sando* is, well, self-explanatory. The cutlet element is a piece of pork or chicken, beaten out and panéed in panko breadcrumbs. It's served with a shredded white cabbage slaw and dressed with two sauces. *Tonkatsu* sauce ('Bull-Dog' brand is best), which is something between a thickened Worcestershire and standard chip shop brown sauce, and Kewpie, the favourite Japanese mayo, which as discussed earlier is a little like salad cream, and is also laden with extra MSG. All of this is served between two slices of *shokupan*.

Shokupan, or the slightly sweeter version called *Hokkaido* milk bread, is the favourite sandwich loaf of Japan (we saw it earlier in the *tamago sando*, page 104). It's made in a similar way to regular white bread but enriched with an egg and powdered milk. Though it uses yeast, it's based on a *tangzhong*, a sort of cooked roux. It's an unfamiliar process to most western bread makers, but it creates a dough that can hold a lot of gas during cooking, becoming fluffy without getting chewy.

Bread is thought to have been introduced to Japan by the Portuguese in the mid-sixteenth century – the Japanese *pan* comes from the Portuguese *pão* – but it remained a bit of an oddity until during the Meiji period (1868–1912) when bakers near naval ports began making double-cooked bread to provision ships and the process quickly industrialised. *Shokupan* – literally, 'eating bread' – came into being after the Second World War, when the US began supplying large quantities of wheat and powdered milk to a nation that had hitherto built most of its diet around rice.

Shokupan, really the very definition of mass-produced packaged bread, is now so much part of the childhood of modern Japanese food lovers that they have the same fondness for it as we have for the loaves we grew up with, and have elevated *shokupan* to their own, extraordinary food pantheon. In 2019, the Japanese electronics company Mitsubishi launched a remarkable high-tech toaster, which closes entirely around a single standard slice of *shokupan* and toasts it to rigorous perfection, keeping track of colour, temperature and humidity in the chamber and calculating timings with an on-board computer. You can own one of these astonishing objects for a mere £350 (about $450), though you'll have to make your own *shokupan* if you want slices that fit.

The *katsu* part of the sando is also a comparatively recent immigrant to Japan. It first appeared at a restaurant called Rengatei in Tokyo in 1899 and may have been inspired by schnitzel sandwiches popular in America. It was certainly associated with *yōshoku*, the trend in Japanese cooking to adapt western recipes.

Today, your *katsu* will sound all the right hipster bells as it arrives at your table. The pork cutlet will probably be rare breed or Ibérico, the chef will probably have whipped up his own take on sweet *tonkatsu* sauce and you can only pray he's had the humility to stick to Kewpie mayonnaise. The *sando* will be cut in a way that screams out to be Instagrammed but, if it's any good, the bread will be, by most of the standards we've learned to call on, 'dreadful'.

A brioche or an artisanal sourdough encompassing the crisp cutlet will not provoke soft tears of nostalgia from a Japanese diner, any more than strips of breaded sea bass in a wasabi mayo would in my own fish finger sandwich.

Two cuts of pork are favoured for the *katsu*. You can slice some fillet (otherwise known as tenderloin), which will give you something incredibly lean, or you can try to replicate the authentic *rosu-katsu*, which is loin with a large slab of delicious fat along one side. To us, this is a standard large pork chop with the bone and rind removed (some supermarkets sell these as 'pork steaks').

Season your meat with salt and pepper, lay it between two layers of greaseproof paper and beat it with a rolling pin until it's a regular 8mm (⅓ inch) thick. Don't worry if it looks huge, as it will shrink back a little on cooking. Lay the beaten meat in plain flour so that both sides are thinly coated. Now dip it into beaten egg and then panko breadcrumbs.

What's really noticeable here is that there are no characteristically Japanese seasonings or treatments involved. No soy, garlic or ginger, no *sanshō* pepper or ground seaweeds… it seems that the very point of both the bread and the meat inside is blandness. Paradoxically, this is not an unusual pattern in many popular street foods. Think for a moment of a Big Mac fresh off the griddle. I defy even the most refined of palates to distinguish any describable taste in the bun, the iceberg lettuce or the patty… it's the sauce that's doing the heavy lifting, and in doing so creates one of the wonders of the culinary world.

There's something about the elegant restraint of the *katsu sando* that makes me want to rebel. I'm also aware that most of the elements in it spring from western cooking. The breadcrumbed cutlet can be a pork chop, the *shokupan* bread can be the western white loaf that inspired it, the Bull-Dog sauce can be the bottled 'brown sauce' from which it descended and Kewpie mayonnaise does taste remarkably like salad cream.

Heat a large knob of butter in a frying pan until it melts and bubbles, then fry your cutlet until golden on both sides. Put to one side to rest on kitchen paper.

Lay out two slices of packaged white bread, then cut the rested cutlet into diagonal slices and lay them out on one slice of the bread. Squeeze on a zigzag pattern of Bull-Dog (or brown sauce), turn the slice 90 degrees and lay on a zigzag pattern of Kewpie mayonnaise (or salad cream). Pile on a handful of shredded white cabbage, apply the lid to the *sando* and trim the crusts off neatly.

Pav Bhaji and Bread Pakora

The Japanese are by no means alone in adapting mass-produced, western-style bread to create something entirely unique. The bread *bhaji*, or bread *pakora*, is a popular street food across the northern parts of India and often appears as a canapé at parties or weddings.

Much like a grilled cheese sandwich in a diner, it's a combination of ingredients that might already be in use in the kitchen for other dishes, but which are infinitely enhanced by frying.

India has a spectacularly broad bread culture, ranging from unleavened flatbreads made from a variety of grains, all the way through to stuffed *naan* and *paratha*. Some are best fresh off the hotplate, some need a while to absorb their rich filling or toppings… but it's hard to see how any of them could be improved upon by the introduction, by colonisers, of a factory-made bland loaf with a long shelf life. Packaged bread, though, soon became popular across India with Anchor, Prince and Modern being the top brands. Perhaps unsurprisingly in such a febrile and creative food culture, it was quickly adopted as an ingredient in home kitchens in other far more interesting ways.

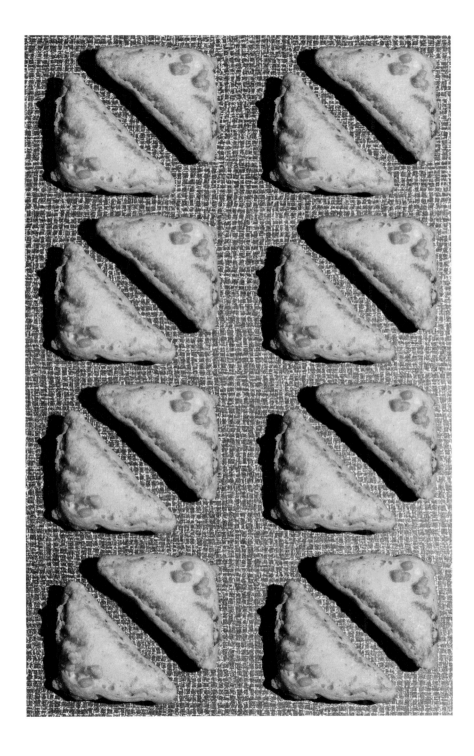

If you've never tried *pav bhaji*, do so now. It's basically boiled potatoes, mashed and refried with a particular spice mix, or masala,[34] fragrant and sour with amchur.[35] Peas and perhaps chopped tomato are added and it's often served from street carts, in hot rolls, dripping with enormous quantities of melted butter. This is in itself a remarkable use of white bread – much to our own disadvantage, we westerners seem too timid about filling bread with carbohydrates[36] – but it pales into insignificance beside the bread pakora.

So let's say, for the sake of argument, you might have some leftover spiced vegetable mix lying around in the kitchen. Surely the simplest thing to do with it would be to cut the crusts off a slice of packaged white bread, spoon some of the mixture on and then fold the bread around it, pinching the doughy material around the edges to seal it. Dip the whole lot in a gram flour batter and fry it.

If you don't have any leftovers – and, let's face it, it's unlikely you will if your family are anything like as greedy as mine or unless you make it in five-kilogram batches – then you can smear the bread with your favourite proprietary Indian pickle and top it with a dollop of plain mash and a sprinkling of garam masala.

This is not, as you can see, a precise science, but it is, I think, the soundest theological argument I've ever encountered for pantheism. *Pav bhaji* and bread *pakora* are so damned good that one god is an insufficient number to praise for their existence.

---

[34] If you're not already a regular and inquisitive customer of your local Indian food shop, then a) I'm astonished b) we can no longer be friends and c) you can order *pav bhaji* masala online.

[35] Powdered, dried sour mango. By itself it will shrivel your face. Applied to vegetables it is a revelation.

[36] There is, of course, the chip butty… but that's another story (see page 73).

Kare Pan

Related in many ways to the bread *pakora* is the Japanese *kare pan* or curry roll, a popular street food with a weird and convoluted relationship to India. It may seem strange that curry is a popular flavouring in Japan, a country with few historical connections with India, and its voyage is a fascinating one.

For many centuries, Japan was an entirely closed society, interaction with foreigners proscribed by law. There was some cultural intersection with China and a little via the few ports where international trade took place, but even these were highly controlled via national trade monopolies.

It was during the Meiji period that the emperor first attempted various forms of westernisation, introducing more democratic government and outlawing feudal customs – including the Samurai, a class of warriors-for-hire who enforced the rule of feudal lords.[37] Emporer Meiji also encouraged the consumption of meat for the first time in what was a largely vegetarian/ pescatarian culture – it is said he did so because he felt that Japanese sailors were physically smaller than the British and American seamen now arriving in the newly opened ports. The conclusion was drawn that eating meat was what distinguished these fine specimens and so it was promoted.

Also popular in the rations of the British navy was 'curry'. Britain occupied India at the time and had taken to eating spicy dishes influenced by Indian cooking. Military doctrine held that curry was not only popular, but a defence against some tropical illnesses. Navy curry wasn't made with any eye to authenticity, just with lots of the branded 'curry powders' that had become favourites amongst returning colonists.

The Japanese navy, following the British custom, began eating '*kare*' every Friday. The 'curry' flavour they adopted at that time has remained a national favourite and is probably the closest thing we'll ever be able to taste to the colonialist's version of 'curry'.

[37] Emperor Meiji outlawed the wearing of the topknot and the carrying of swords – the two symbols of the Samurai. In doing so he forced a generation of skilled sword makers to turn their skills to culinary knives, creating the tradition of superb Japanese blades. Someone should write a book about this stuff.

Japanese *kare* isn't made with judicious blends of spices, fresh from the *dabba*, but from a flavoured roux. It can be made from scratch by frying curry powder and flour in oil or it can be bought ready-made in blocks – which need only hot water and a slow stir to turn into a thick sauce.

Kare pan comprises a curried vegetable filling, usually potato, wrapped in bread dough and either baked as a rather sophisticated and glossy bun, or rolled in panko breadcrumbs and deep-fried. As promised, a full circle back to the bread pakora.

The filling is simple. Just peel a few potatoes, a carrot and an onion, and cut them into small dice. Gently fry the onions in a little oil, then add the potatoes and carrot and a little water and simmer gently. Don't use salt to season, stick to soy sauce. Stir in a large spoonful of the sort of curry powder you wouldn't use for a curry, but which you might consider for an authentically 1950s coronation chicken. We're talking school curry here – definitely nothing authentic. Alternatively, dissolve a Japanese curry sauce block in some boiling water and then pour over the vegetables. Continue simmering until the vegetables are soft and the curry is dry. We don't need anything like a wet 'gravy'.

Make up a simple bread dough with plain flour, instant yeast, warm milk and softened butter, then knead the dough thoroughly – it's easiest with a dough hook. The dough should be rested until it doubles in size, then it can be rolled out into discs. Put a spoonful of the cooled *kare* mixture into the centre of each disc, draw up the edges and seal into a ball if you're going for buns, or a kind of pasty shape if you want to deep-fry it.

If you're making the buns, they should be allowed another forty-five minutes or so to rise before egg washing and baking, while the semi-circular pasties can be dipped in egg wash and panko breadcrumbs and then given half an hour or so to rest before frying until puffed up and brown.

Damp Sandwiches

I grew up by the sea. People always imagine that means a kind of *Famous Five* childhood of brown skin, tousled hair and endless picnics and, to be fair, there were plenty of picnics. But I don't remember wicker hampers, roast chickens and tartan blankets on rolling green downs. I remember fighting for a space in a car park and then getting loaded like a packhorse with buckets, bags, Thermos flasks and gallon plastic jugs of sickly squash. I remember Dad sweating and cursing under a mare's nest of pointy sticks and bright striped neon, wrestling with the windbreaks and, for some reason, a set of plastic boules.

There was never a good spot nearby; it was always over the next endless dune. An interminable hot trek, feet slipping in boiling sand and, unlike Lawrence of Arabia, without a convenient intermission. Eventually our spirits would break before we could find a good spot, so we'd settle for three square metres, miraculously free of dog deposits but not quite far enough away from the couple trying energetically to consummate under a small towel. We slumped to the ground and only then were able to contemplate the horror of the sandwiches.

The sandy sandwich has been a staple of music hall comedians since the advent of the bathing machine, but the feeling of grit between the molars is the least of the textural atrocities in a picnic sarnie. Where a French or Italian peasant will whip out a loaf, filling and a pocketknife and create something perfectly lovely while sat in a hedgerow, the British have always felt the need to make sandwiches hours in advance. An authentic British picnic sandwich is assembled from wet ingredients and processed bread, hermetically sealed in foil or film and incubated until it reduces to a sweaty, homogenous mulch. Even now, the image of a slice of overripe beef tomato embedded in a piece of warm Wonderloaf and topped with a dispiriting sheet of perspiring Cheddar is enough to provoke neurasthenic flashbacks.

You must remember picnic sandwiches, too. They form a sort of collective mental scar that we'll never really heal. You *know* what a slice of overripe tomato looks like when it's been mashed into a slice of packaged white bread. You *know* how the juices bleach the waxy yellow block Cheddar to the colour of a drowned man's skin. You *know* what happens to all of it when it's wrapped in cling film to incubate and then liberally sprinkled with dirty grey sand. We all know… we were all there.

It is, therefore, no wonder that a normal English person is appalled, even nauseated by the idea of a wet, warm sandwich – how could we not be? Yet across the world there is a family, a class of sandwiches that is designed to be served hot and damp, and all are the better for it. What follows might be difficult to read in places, but we should be brave and dive in.

The Pan Bagnat

If you've ever asked for a sandwich in France, you'd be forgiven for thinking they had a pretty weak game nationally. Baguette/butter/ham and baguette/butter/cheese are often claimed as part of the *faites simple* philosophy of food, but can often seem deeply unimaginative and, dare I say it, dull. Sure, if the three ingredients are each exceptional, the results can be pleasing, but almost anyone less hidebound by culinary tradition will be aware that it could be enhanced by a spot of pickle or a handful of crisp lettuce and a splurt of mayo.

No… it would be a justified accusation, that is, until you order a sandwich in Nice or the surrounding areas. For it is there that the French have cast aside all their own rules and created a sandwich of such magnificence that I swear they don't know what to do with it.

First take a large baguette or boule that you've allowed to stale for a day and split it in half. As we've seen in other recipes, staling the bread makes it more able to absorb liquids and also makes the cut surface rough and abrasive. Rub, therefore, both cut faces with a peeled clove of garlic, then hose both sides with the most expensive olive oil to which you have access. Open a can of good-quality tuna in olive oil, drain off the oil into a bowl

and lay the tuna in big flakes on the oily bread. Add a smear of Dijon mustard, a splash of sherry vinegar and some salt and pepper to the tuna oil to make a rudimentary dressing, then toss in some pitted black olives, sliced red onion, blanched green beans, chunks of tomato and lettuce leaves. Layer everything on top of the tuna, sprinkle on a few capers if you really want to inflame the traditionalists, and perhaps a few anchovies, then pour the remaining dressing over everything. Finally, top with a layer of sliced hard-boiled eggs – the 'fudgy' consistency outlined earlier (see page 103) – and close up the loaf.

Now squish down the top until things start to get messy and then wrap the whole thing in several layers of cling film. Arrange the loaf upside down on a plate, weight it down with a heavy pan or some tins and leave in the fridge overnight.

Remove the sandwich from the fridge several hours before you plan to eat it so that it can come up to a suitably Côte d'Azur temperature throughout and the various oils have a chance to become liquid again and further soak everything.

Now, you could argue that for someone in Nice to stick their famous local salad (minus the spuds) in a loaf of bread and squash it doesn't display the kind of culinary inventiveness we've come to expect from French cooks, but you'd be wrong, because it's the blending – the interplay, if you will – of the elements that makes this sandwich greater than the sum of its parts.

The Meatball Sub

The messiest sandwich known to science is the meatball marinara, which has only lost a little of its popularity since beards became fashionable in parts of New York. There is something about getting garlicky, oily tomato sauce in your facial hair that's difficult to live with – and particularly difficult to share with your beloved.

The marinara is a 'sub', sold as a takeaway snack from small restaurants that might, at other times of the day, offer the same meatballs over a bowl of spaghetti. The restaurateur will love them because they're cheap and easy to keep hot on the counter for a whole day's service or longer. The customer loves them because… well, you be the judge.

Mix together some beef mince with fennel-flavoured *salsiccia*, skins removed, in roughly equal quantities. Add a healthy handful of stale Italian breadcrumbs, a dollop of crème fraîche and a beaten egg. Season immoderately with salt, black pepper, grated fresh garlic, garlic powder, fennel seeds and a little dried oregano. Form the mixture into balls the size of large eggs.

Now make a very simple tomato sauce. Start with a couple of tins of decent tomatoes and three or four peeled cloves of garlic. Place it all in a shallow oven dish and roast, uncovered, on a high setting until the top starts to scorch. Then liquidise the sauce with an immersion blender and season with salt, pepper and lots of olive oil. Use a little less salt than you feel tastes perfect. Drop in the meatballs, cover the dish and allow it to sit, barely simmering, on top of the stove for as long as you can. The idea is to replicate food sitting on a steam table on a deli counter for a long day's service, during which time the insides of the meatballs will poach gently while the outside will share its flavours with a slowly reducing sauce.

When you can bear it no longer, half split an undistinguished white roll. Something about half the length of a baguette, firm enough to take a soaking, but soft enough not to put up much resistance to the teeth.

Lift two or three of the meatballs out of the sauce and lay them in the roll. Top with slices of provolone and ladle over a load of sauce. If the cheese doesn't show sufficient signs of compliance, it can be encouraged to melt by flashing it under a grill.

The finished sandwich should not fit easily into your mouth in any direction. Serve with a spare clean shirt.

The French Dip

Perhaps the wettest sandwich of all came into being in Los Angeles, on a date still hotly disputed by the two restaurants that lay claim to inventing it. Cole's[38] claim to have served the French dip when they opened in 1908, while Philippe's[39] claim to have invented it in 1918.

The French dip is a roast beef sandwich on a 'French' baguette-style roll that's been dipped in the juices from the meat roasting pan. At Philippe's, the roll is cut and immersed in a tank of beefy liquid before assembly; at Cole's, the juice comes in a bowl so that the customer can judge precisely how soaked he wants his bread. It's a simple idea, though both establishments have created competing and ever-changing origin myths about servers accidentally dropping rolls in the gravy jug, off-duty cops or firefighters ordering the dip to soften rolls that had staled during the long day and even a customer with bad teeth who needed his sandwich soaked. All or none of these may have basis in truth, as the idea of dipping bread in gravy is hardly the most outrageous innovation, given that a big chunk of meat in a pan of delicious juices is sitting out on the counter.

[38] Cole's Pacific Electric Buffet. 118 East 6th Street, Los Angeles.
[39] Philippe the Original. 1001 N Alameda Street, Los Angeles.

The problem with the French dip, as any keen cook will already have spotted, is in the mathematics. A large joint will produce many thin slices of delicious roast beef, but nowhere near enough juices to soak everyone's baguette.

At this point, a mysterious product from the food wholesaler makes its appearance – canned *au jus* (French for 'with juice', but pronounced by the counterman 'aw joo'). It's got about as much to do with the juices from the meat on the counter as Bovril does with your Sunday roast, but '*au jus*' is poured with abandon anywhere in the US that hot roast beef sandwiches are served.

Without the canned beef essence it can be tough to get the proper French dip experience. Even a properly made and well-reduced beef stock doesn't quite hit the spot, and anything more heavily worked begins to taste like gravy, which has a whole other set of ramifications for the British sandwich lover.[40]

If you want to make your own French dip, you'll need a hot roast beef joint from which to shave the thinnest possible slices, and you'll need to save any drippings as you slice. To achieve the texture and the almost hyper-beefiness of '*au jus*', the closest thing will be canned beef consommé, if you can still find such a thing on the shelves of your supermarket or deli. It's usually stored next to the exotic soups, nestled between tinned lobster bisque and *soupe de poisson* in sealed jars. It will be heavily undersalted, but that can easily be corrected, and the juices from the joint will round out the flavour. It's important not to mess with it further, though, or you'll be dipping your sandwich in a cheffy broth and that would be quite contrary to the spirit of the thing. The dip shouldn't be thickened, as that would make it cling unattractively to the surface of the bread rather than soaking in quickly, though it would be nice if it had a gelatinous quality from the consommé.

[40] I refer, of course, to that triumph of north-eastern culinary arts, the stottie. This is a specially made bread, halfway between a small loaf and a very large roll, soft in texture but with a substantial and strong crust, the better to hold its shape when packed with sliced roast beef and drenched in gravy. The beef stottie is proof – should it be required – that God is a Geordie; but it is not a French dip.

The Lampredotto

The first time I went to Florence was as an art student in the 1980s. I spent some time as an assistant to a photographer, then spent days wandering the streets with a diminishing stock of Lire and Tri-X film.

Early one morning I found myself in the Mercato Centrale – it's quite gentrified these days, but back then it was a genuinely scuzzy wholesale food market. Wandering foodies are always attracted to markets for the simple reason that the places the traders eat invariably have the best breakfasts at the lowest prices. I found myself drawn by the gravitational pull of Da Nerbone, a stall with a huge queue. This, it turned out, was for the *lampredotto*, a local sandwich comprising a soft roll packed with hot sauce and the long, slow-braised third stomach of a cow. Yep – tripe in a bun. It's a lot better than it sounds. And though I can't replicate the student hunger that made it taste so sublime, I've been back in the last couple of years and the same family are still serving it. The queue hasn't diminished one bit.

You queue to buy a ticket with a mix of locals, tourists and stallholders. At the counter you try to communicate, in front of an increasingly hostile crowd, that yes, you do want the tripe and yes, you know what it is and no, you wouldn't prefer the beef. If all else fails, resort to gesture and grunt. Ticket obtained, you now join an even longer queue to reach the *Lampredotto* Guy.

The *Lampredotto* Guy has clearly been doing it all his life, except, according to the slogan on his hat, when he is at the Firenze boxing club. He is very, very good with the tripe, though, judging by his nose, not so good at the boxing. Taking up a huge knife, he slashes open a semi-crusty bread roll, then uses the tip to fish around in the tank visible to his left for a flubbery slab of greige tripe and slap it onto a board. He stares at you from under the mass of scar tissue that forms his brow in silent challenge: 'Have you any idea what this is, fool?'

He minces the tripe with one hand while dipping the bottom of the bap into the *fluids* in the tank, then assembles everything while gesticulating with the knife. It is a relief to realise that he's actually asking you to choose between a lurid green and a lurid red sauce, either of which may well contain enough capsaicin to subdue a prison riot.

He applies your sauce, wraps the bun in greaseproof paper and thrusts it at you, dropping the shoulder, taking the weight on the back leg and driving through in a tight upward swing.

It is stunningly good. Rich, long-cooked fatty connective tissue. It looks and tastes like the kind of stuff that people get all disgusted about if you don't remove it from a stew, and so have to eat it quietly afterwards in the kitchen. It's a treat not to have to hide while eating it.

We could try, if you like, to work out a recipe between us, though how we could replicate the soft, unsalted roll from the bakery next door, I'm not sure. With a bathtub and a fire hose, we could work our way through the long scrubbing of the stomach, which, to my admittedly warped judgement, seems to be about the size of a modest single duvet cover made of wet rubber and smelling aggressively of the byre. I suppose we could rig up some sort of heated bucket and cook it for a day or two, if we were ready to stay up late watching it simmer like a primordial tar pit, honking like a midden. Maybe we could fake the sauces... but there's no way on God's Earth we could imitate the *sprezzatura* of the delivery or the press of honest, hungry tripe enthusiasts in the crowded market. Buy a ticket to Florence. Say the Englishman sent you.

The Railroad Sandwich

It's never inappropriate to quote my literary hero MFK Fisher, but this is perhaps one of her least sensually erotic suggestions with food – what was referred to in her family as 'the railroad sandwich'.

She describes making a sandwich much like the aforementioned, but adds this crucial instruction for an extra phase of 'cooking':

Put the two halves firmly together, and wrap them loosely in plastic or foil or wax paper, and then a clean towel. Then, and this is the Secret Ingredient, call upon a serene onlooker (a broad or at least positive beam adds to the quick results, and here I do not refer to a facial grimace but to what in other dialects is called a behind-derriere-bum... etc.), to sit gently but firmly upon this loaf for at least twenty minutes.[41]

[41] From *With Bold Knife and Fork* (1968), a collection of pieces Fisher wrote for *The New Yorker*.

With & From Bread

Age Cannot Wither...

Bread is a perishable product and we refer to the process of its degradation as 'staling'. Because fresh bread is usually moist and soft, we assume that stale bread has simply dried out – that its moisture has evaporated – but this is only a very small part of the story. How bread stales and how we control that process is a contributing factor to most of our bread traditions, beliefs and recipes.

The texture of the 'crumb' – the body of the bread as distinct from the outer crust – is a result of the starch in flour gelatinising. This is a structural change, whereby the bonds between molecules are broken down by water and heat in such a way that the starch can engage more water, forming a gel.[42]

Bread will stale when, over time, the gel breaks down, releasing water and allowing the starch to recrystallise. It's a fine distinction to make, given that the result seems very much like dried-out bread – the important thing to realise is that staling will still occur in non-drying conditions. The breaking down of the gelatinised starch occurs faster at just above freezing point, so bread will stale faster if kept in the fridge.

If bread has gone stale, it can be partially brought back to life by applying heat again, causing some of the starch and water to re-gel, but it will stale doubly quickly as it cools down, so reheating is usually just a rescue trick for tired baguettes at dinner parties.

Wrapping bread tightly in an airtight material *does* prevent evaporation, but the moisture retained is absorbed by the much drier crust of the loaf. When unwrapped, the crumb might seem to have been 'preserved', but the crust will have lost its crispness and achieved an unpleasant leathery texture.

---

[42] A gel is a colloidal substance: a semi-solid created when a solid is dispersed in a liquid.

Dampness is an enemy to good bread, as it encourages mould. Fresh bread, without preservatives, left exposed to the air at room temperature will stale before mould ever gets a chance to grow. Tightly wrapped bread may grow mould before it seems 'dried out' – but machine-produced bread, specially treated to avoid degelatinisation of the starch, and wrapped in an airtight bag, will grow a luxurious pelt of multicoloured moulds while, at least technically, not staling.

The best way to keep bread fresh is to keep it at room temperature in something that protects it but isn't entirely airtight – something through which it can 'breathe'. The paper bag in which you brought it home from the baker is a good start, or the traditional wrapping for commercial loaves, a sort of loose wax paper wrapping, does the trick, too. A traditional 'bread bin' will keep it in good nick for as long as it decently can, and several companies now sell a reusable food-wrap material made of light cotton fabric coated in beeswax that seems to do the job wonderfully. Personally I favour a canvas bag. This keeps the crumb in good condition for as long as possible, maintains crispness in the crust and means that any leftover pieces are untroubled by moulds once they actually do go stale – at which point they can be used in any one of hundreds of recipes calling for stale bread.

The best way to have great, fresh bread on hand at all times is to use your freezer. Fresh bread, with its moisture locked up in starch gel, freezes brilliantly. Slice the loaf as soon as you get it home, have your first meal out of it, then bag it and freeze it as soon as possible. For weeks to come you'll be able to take the loaf from the freezer and crack off a slice or two (use a palette knife please, not a sharp one, if the slices need to be coaxed apart), which will defrost in minutes and taste as good as the day they were baked. This also makes it possible to have half a dozen different types of bread available at all times.

Making things with leftover bread is kind of a private ritual. It's done in family kitchens, often during difficult times. Recipes become loaded with complicated emotions and deeply loved. If 'recipes' are ever passed on, it would be orally or in a handwritten note – so it's sometimes surprising when one comes into the public domain.

I have on my shelf a strange old book called *As We Like It: Cookery Recipes by Famous People*. It was published in 1950 and proceeds from its sale went to a charity for returning prisoners of war. The list of contributors is vast and ranges from The Dowager Marchioness of Reading, GBE, CStJ to George Bernard Shaw. Some of the recipes are short and homely like the one supplied by Cicely Courtneidge for 'Prawns Spécialité' (with tomato, cucumber and salad dressing), or complex and ostentatious like the Provençal fish preparation by Richard Burton and Elizabeth Taylor, which is clearly designed to announce not just their fabulous home on the Riviera but also the presence of a world-class private chef.

It's an entertaining snapshot of the era – of a nation just coming out of rationing and becoming what we'd now see as 'aspirational', impressed by new stars yet still displaying immense deference to a traditional aristocracy. My favourite of all the recipes, though, is this…

White bread
Cream
Grated cheese
Pepper

Cut stale white bread into fingers. Soak in cream. Then roll in Parmesan cheese and pepper and pat with a knife so the cheese sticks well. Butter baking-sheet and bake in a very hot oven and turn when one side is brown, so that the other side browns.

Serve very hot.

You can do this with grated Cheddar or Gruyère if you have no Parmesan. The fingers should be crisp on the outside, and soft and creamy inside.

These still taste completely delicious and work as an excellent savoury, particularly when you solemnly introduce them as 'Winston Churchill's Cheesy Fingers'.

Eggy Breads

After we've learned to make toast, the first thing most kids tackle in the kitchen is some form of 'eggy bread'. It would be wrong to dignify it, at this stage, with the term French toast because it's too simple. The bread's job is to hold the egg in position while it cooks, like an omelette, but with less chasing it around the pan… less to go wrong. I vividly remember cooking my first slice and the thrill of turning something out of a pan and onto a plate, a feeling that stays with me to this day. Eggy bread was the first thing my daughter cooked, too. It isn't just taking a piece of bread out of a packet and sticking it in a toaster – this, however simple, is the first step in Proper Cooking.

Just as simple is the Jewish breakfast favourite, *matzo brei*… a dish that frankly involves even less preparation. *Matzo* is an unleavened bread, something like a cracker, that comes in big square sheets. It's crumbled into milk or water and allowed to soak for a couple of minutes until it's soft, then scrambled into eggs – one egg per sheet of *matzo*. The ideal frying/scrambling medium is *schmaltz* (chicken fat), and it works well with a little salt, maybe ketchup or, if you're feeling really crazy, some chopped chives or spring onion. Alternatively, the whole thing can be subverted with sugar or honey and a sprinkling of cinnamon, under which circumstances butter is the appropriate fat.

I've still got a soft spot for the very simplest iteration of eggy bread: a slice quickly flipped in beaten egg and fried in a pan. The egg forms a thin, omelettey layer on the soft, warm bread. If you cut it into thin fingers or cubes before dipping, you can up the egg/bread ratio. It's probably best with ketchup. But it's also just a starting point.

Pain perdu is what the French call French toast. It's more elegant, richer and takes a little more work. You can start with brioche, a bread already fortified with eggs and butter, but the important thing is not the eggy skin but the custard texture of the interior. The eggs should be beaten with a little cream, to effectively slow down the setting process, sweetened with sugar and flavoured with Grand Marnier and vanilla – and the bread should be allowed to soak thoroughly. No matter how thick you cut your slices, you need the egg mixture to soak right through to the centre.

Fry the first side in clarified butter and pour a little more of the egg mixture onto the top – just to make sure it's completely soaked – then flip it. It doesn't need to be more than lightly tanned on the outside, but the idea is that the interior should just set. Thick pieces can be kept in a warm oven for a while, but the best way to be sure of perfection is to use a probe thermometer and cook to a core temperature of 70°C (158°F).

Served carefully, dusted with icing sugar and cinnamon, it's a dessert worthy of the poshest French restaurant… but it's not quite the best version it can be.

Speculaas Pain Perdu

Speculaas butter might just be one of the most dangerous ingredients on the planet. *Speculaas* are small, spiced biscuits, common all over Scandinavia and northern Europe and traditionally baked around Christmas time. Their flavouring varies, but they usually include a fair amount of ginger, some cardamom and that particular cinnamon they favour in Scandinavian baking that's softer and a little less honkingly fragrant than the 'pumpkin spice' preferred in other countries. Weirdly, they have become popular worldwide since airline caterers started serving them with coffee. We taste things differently on planes, but the particular flavour of the 'European cookie' somehow fixed in the minds of travellers. It's thought that Lotus Foods, one of the largest manufacturers of the biscuits, was the first to blend them into a buttery spread, which soon achieved a kind of cult status all over the world.[43]

[43] Lotus sell the biscuits and spread under the name Biscoff in some countries.

If you can't get your hands on *speculaas* biscuits, a few standard ginger biscuits will do. Crumble them into a blender with a similar quantity of chilled, unsalted butter and season with a pinch of salt, a shake of ground cardamom and some ground cassia. Blitz everything to a smooth consistency and pack into a jar. Take a single, thick slice of white bread and, using a sharp knife, split it in half laterally, leaving one edge uncut. You could also use the point of the knife to cut a pocket instead, but either way it's important to leave the slices connected. Thickly smear the flavoured butter between the slices, then gently press them back together. At this point you can freeze the prepared slices or store them, wrapped, overnight in the fridge.

When you're ready to eat, dip the slice in an egg wash, well beaten with just a little cream or milk (you don't want to weaken it too far, but it's important that it's runny enough to soak in). You can season the egg a little if you wish, but the flavoured butter should do most of the work. Fry both sides in clarified butter and serve dusted with icing sugar. The *speculaas* butter will have melted into the bread from the inside and will be held in place by the egg coating. The biscuit crumbs might hold a pleasant crunch, or, if you're lucky, they'll have homogenised into an entirely smooth paste. Either way, you should eat this on a hotel balcony, overlooking Copenhagen harbour on a crisp autumn morning.

Wet Bread

Sogginess in bread is something we all fear. Damp toast is depressing, a wet sandwich is deeply polarising and there's something approaching nauseating about the texture of a slice of bread that has somehow got wet. It may have been placed on an improperly dried plate or too close to a glass dripping with condensation, but when bread soaks up water it feels wrong in the mouth. Yet intentionally using wet bread, particularly when it's staled and extra absorbent, is the first step in using it as an ingredient.

Once we've overcome our fear of wet bread, a world of wonder is open to us. There's a whole string of recipes from all round the world in which stale bread is included in salads, partly as a filling element but more usually as an absorbent vehicle for dressing. *Paximadia* are Greek barley rusks that are double cooked so that they last pretty much forever. In a seafaring nation, they probably originated as a hardtack-style biscuit – indeed, they can be served just soaked in water to reconstitute them, but are best broken up and sprinkled into a *horiatiki*-style salad. If there's plenty of oil and lemon juice in the dressing, it will soften the bread by itself and the dark, nutty nature of the barley adds a whole new level of depth to the salad.

Panzanella

Moving further around the Mediterranean, we encounter *panzanella*, the Italian salad that uses great chunks of stale bread. Italian bread, particularly the ideal Tuscan *pan sciocco*, stales quickly and is usually undersalted to our taste, so it is absolutely ideal for the job of soaking up dressing… and more. The secret to a great *panzanella* is to disobey the near-unbreakable rule of salad making and to start dressing it way ahead of serving. The edict from St Elizabeth David about dressing only at the very last minute

with 'lashings of good olive oil' and scant vinegar is very sensible if you don't want lettuce leaves to wilt in seconds to an unappetising mulch, but *panzanella* should begin hours beforehand with raw onions and salt.

Raw onions can be a bit fierce in a salad, but the oxalic acid in them – the stuff that makes us weep and gag – is trapped in plump cells on the surface and is released when the cells are disrupted. It's why you cry more when grating onions or chopping them with a blunt knife – more cells are crushed, and more acid is sprayed out. You can tame onions by blanching them in boiling water, but there's a much cleverer trick that Turkish cooks favour when making their amazing *ezme* salad.[44]

Place some sliced onions into a salad bowl and pour over the same amount of coarse-grained salt you might eventually expect to use in the dressing. Now, using your hands (in latex gloves if you ever want to be accepted in polite company again), scrunch up the onions and salt with vicious enthusiasm. The sharp salt crystals will cut into the surface of the onions, releasing loads of oxalic acid into the air and a sweetly flavoured onion juice into the bowl. Sure, you, the cook, will weep like you've been tear-gassed, but this will pass, and your dining companions will experience only the best part of the onion.

The onion juice is, of course, laden with salt, so it's now time to toss in your chopped, ripe tomatoes. These need to be juicy, even a little overripe isn't a problem, and most emphatically not deseeded. The minute they hit that salt they're going to start weeping juice – a dreadful solecism in a polite side salad but vital to a gutsy *panzanella*. Add a little more salt – trust me, it will work – and now, if you're brave, you can put the bowl in the fridge overnight and let it really collapse.

When it's time to assemble your salad, things go quite back to normal. You can chop some red and yellow sweet peppers if you need them, some cucumber if you are so inclined, rip up some basil leaves in preparation and have ready some capers and an anchovy or two. When you take your salad out of the fridge, you'll have some onions and tomatoes effectively swimming in a highly flavoured liquid, which is, of course, the base of the dressing. Grate or crush some garlic according to your taste and smush up

[44] Made most impressively at L'As du Fallafel, 34 rue des Rosiers, Paris – which isn't even Turkish.

an anchovy. Add these to the juice with a couple of glugs of white wine vinegar and taste. Now start adding olive oil until the dressing comes into balance. You can add a little sugar and black pepper if needed.

Look at the bowl. If there's a really absurd amount of liquid in there, just chuck in great hunks of stale bread. If you fear there isn't enough juice, you could soak the bread in water for two minutes, then wring it out before adding it to the salad. Either way, it now needs to stand for a good fifteen minutes before it gets served, which will give you ample time to add some capers, or some shards of black olive if you're feeling feisty and iconoclastic, and finally to adjust the seasoning and give everything the occasional stir.

By the time it hits the table, each chunk of bread should be soaked through properly with all the flavours we associate with Tuscany, the vegetable ingredients should be modestly dressed in flavoured oil and the bottom of the bowl should contain little, if any, juice.

Gazpacho

You would think that the Spanish, with their fine appreciation of all things tomato and bread, would have an equivalent bread salad to the *panzanella*, but no – with fiendish cunning, they've evolved something arguably better and, if anything, even more cooling on a boiling-hot day.

Take each of the ingredients of the *panzanella* above and, in the same order, add them to a blender. You might want to up the garlic, you may want to omit the olives, maybe swap in some sherry vinegar for the white wine stuff and you will definitely feel inclined to add more olive oil, but you will have created an absolutely authentic gazpacho.

Some argue that bread isn't part of a 'true' gazpacho, but it has the quality of keeping more oil in suspension in the liquid and, in the rural corners of Andalucia where gazpacho originates – where there are few written recipes but a love of oil – I feel that its inclusion is probably appreciated.

If there is one culinary culture that's done more work on stale bread than any other, it must be the Spanish. The remarkable combination of creativity, thrift and a deep appreciation of the delicious means there are thousands of ways with bread in the Spanish repertoire, many of them without recipe or name. At the root of this is the conceptual leap that small pieces of bread are an ingredient in themselves, not just a waste product to be 'used up'. These pieces of bread, called *migas*, can be used as a thickening agent, to replace the starch in most dishes or can be sprinkled over others. *Migas* absorb olive oil in staggering quantities and hoover up the flavour of garlic or herbs while retaining a crunchy texture. In that form, they can be used in the same way as an Italian *gremolata*, to garnish and enhance, or, made in larger pieces, they can form the backbone of a simple dish, topped with a fried egg or shot through with chopped tomatoes and onions. In a place where rice, pasta or potatoes might be expensive or unobtainable, *migas*, in some form or another, can replace any of them.

Upma

Upma is a thick porridge, and is a popular breakfast in southern India. It's traditionally made by toasting semolina or ground rice in a dry pan and then using it to soak up a rich, spiced sauce… you're ahead of me here, aren't you? Yes, as packaged bread has gained popularity across India, a bread-based *upma* has evolved. It's amazing stuff, particularly on a ferocious hangover, as it gives those of us truly unimpressed by yoghurt, fruit or cereal the opportunity to enjoy what is effectively curried toast.

Slip a couple of slices of white bread into a dry pan and toast both sides very lightly – this stiffens up the bread and makes the next stage easier. Now, either slice the bread into neat little cubes or, if you're feeling very hungover, just tear it into small pieces and then toss it back into the pan. Keep the pan moving over the heat until the bread pieces are toasted to a rusk-like consistency, then tip them out onto a plate. Keep the pieces distributed, uncovered and in a single layer so that they can steam off any remaining moisture and not go soggy.

Now brown a few peanuts or cashews in the dry pan. Keep your eyes on the nuts, as they go from perfectly brown to utterly torched in a microsecond.

Next put some mustard oil into the hot pan (or plain vegetable oil if you don't have a fantastic Indian shop nearby – in which case you should move house) and start things off with some mustard seeds, cumin seeds and curry leaves. Don't let things burn, but let them have a proper seeing to, until the seeds begin to spit, before adding some grated ginger, garlic and a good handful of chopped onions. Lower the heat and let everything sweat while you chop up a couple of tomatoes and a fresh green chilli. Add these, plus a splash of water, and let everything cook down until it's soft.

Once the masala looks good – well-combined and still quite fluid – and you've adjusted the seasoning with sugar and salt, you can throw in the toasted bread and stir until it's taken up any loose liquid. Serve with chopped coriander (for health) and a freshly blended mango lassi – or possibly a Bloody Mary. It might just benefit from a fried egg, and once – I believe mezcal was involved – I made an emergency bread *upma* and sprinkled Bombay mix over the top of it.

Nobody died.

Açorda

Aficionados rave about *ribollita*, the bread soup of Tuscany, but to me it seems almost fraudulent in its effortlessness. In spite of long and involved recipes from food writers star-struck by the poetry of the Italian countryside and the romance of tradition, it is basically last night's minestrone with chunks of stale bread in it. Admittedly, most British households might not have leftover minestrone unless someone left their Cup a Soup to go cold in front of the telly the previous night, but seriously Italy, sort yourselves out. *Ribollita* just means 'boiled up again', so claiming it's 'all that' is like the Brits making a big song and dance out of constructing a sarnie out of Sunday lunch leftovers.[45]

Perhaps more considered are the *açordas* of Portugal, which vary hugely in flavour depending on the region and available ingredients, but seem to agree on a) the addition of coriander b) being enriched with egg c) having a truly slurry-like texture in which the bread loses all structural integrity.

A simple *açorda* start with some *toucinho* (smoked bacon) or *chouriço* sausage for flavour, sweated in olive oil. Once there's enough fat in the pan to be worthwhile, add garlic, chopped chilli and the stems of your coriander and lower the heat so that everything breaks down slowly, softening rather than browning. Once you feel you've liberated the flavours, add a lot of good-quality chicken stock to the pan and allow to simmer for a while, then add stale bread, roughly torn and with the crusts. Keep the heat low and stir regularly until the bread has completely broken down into the consistency of a sloppy porridge or a really, frighteningly authentic risotto – this will take about half an hour and you might need to top up the stock to maintain the right consistency.

Finally, take the soup off the heat and allow it to stand for a few minutes before quickly stirring in a couple of beaten eggs. If you do it fast, they won't scramble, but if they do, no one's going to come round and tell you off. Tear up the remaining coriander to top off the serving bowl and, perhaps, to distract from the fact that this is a far less photogenic dish than its deliciousness deserves.

---

[45] Although, now I think about it, that's not a bad national dish to be proud of.

Açordas are so varied that it's unwise to specify any single one. In truth, it's a method more than a recipe. Coastal regions, for example, favour fish *açordas*, using a stock made from trimmings and topped with grilled fish, or served with prawns and made with the water in which they were boiled. Some recipes add plenty of tomato early on so that the bread is effectively soaking in a runny tomato sauce. It's fair to say that anything you might consider doing to a risotto would work well in an *açorda*, and then a whole bunch of other stuff, too.

French Onion Soup

Of all the wet bread soups, French onion is probably the most famous. Like many classics of French provincial cooking, it's probably an urbanised refinement of a much older peasant dish – a dish that almost certainly resembled *açorda*.

Also, like many dishes in the repertoire, it takes advantage of ingredients that would be made in bulk in a professional kitchen and which would feature as sub-ingredients in many other dishes. The best French onion soup would need long-sweated and reduced onions, topped up with a good stock and a shot of booze and then topped with a piece of stale bread and a handful of grated cheese before flashing under a salamander and serving. What's most noticeable here is that this 'classic' of French cuisine could be thrown together by a chef in less time than a hamburger, though replicating the effect at home – where we don't have the pre-made ingredients in large buckets – is a long and involved process.

You won't have a small brigade in your kitchen, so, unfortunately, getting the basic stock right is going to take a while. Days before you plan to make your soup, you're going to need to start with a good chicken stock. You can, if you wish, use the carcass, trim, pan juices and leftovers of a roast chicken, and you could buy a bag of wing tips and bones from your butcher, or, if you're really committed and very organised, you could save the cooking water from a poached chicken.

I know that sounds extravagant, but it's one of the unspoken secrets of the French kitchen. If you poach a chicken – a classic *poule au pot* – you're left with the beginnings of an amazing stock. And what's going to really bake your noodle is how that stock makes the perfect base for a *pot-au-feu*... and then how the liquid from the *pot-au-feu* makes the perfect starting point for FOS.

OK. I completely understand that no modern family that doesn't own half of Yorkshire is going to eat like that in an average week, but it does give you an insight into how a thrifty brasserie owner might be managing his ingredient costs. The canonical brasserie menu is such for a reason. There's a complex web of interactions behind the scenes that gives the best selection of dishes, with the minimum of ingredients shared between them. Nothing goes to waste and the FOS is the ultimate in 'using up'.

Chicken stock is useful because it has richness, but the flavours are subtle and can easily be altered. However, you'll probably want your eventual soup to have a good level of beefiness, so next you'll need to poach some short ribs or other good, strong-flavoured beef cuts in the stock.[46] Roast the meat first in order to darken the colour of your stock and, if you need more gelatine to improve the texture, consider using some oxtail, too.

Now your stock is strong and beefy, it will set when you put it in the fridge, and you'll be able to lift off the fat as a solid cap.[47] It's been hard work, but you're now at the stage you would have been if you were from a wealthy French provincial family in around 1890 with a private cook.

Next turn to the onions. It's now a well-documented fact that caramelising onions takes longer than anyone is prepared to admit in print, but, unfortunately, FOS cannot happen without it. You'll need far more onions than you think – probably two large ones per serving won't be too much. You might think your knife skills are up to thinly slicing that many, but, honestly, for consistency and speed, it's worth getting out the mandoline or the slicing attachment on a food processor.

---

[46] Although a departure from the canon, a FOS made with a strong chicken broth is no bad thing.

[47] For the love of God don't throw it away. You can toast the bread crouton if you wish, but – and I only dare say this in a footnote where the obsessives will find it – it's even better if you fry it in the beef fat.

Prescribed methods for onion caramelisation are as disparate as the imaginations of cooks and, once you've managed a method that works once, you are likely to cleave to it with the terrifying enthusiasm of a zealot and to scorn all alternatives. I reckon the way I do it is a lot less fuss than most and has never failed me yet, but for the sake of all our sanities in these trying times, I offer it in a spirit of kindness and you can take it or, in a very real way, leave it. Don't @ me.

Most methods suggest an initial stage of sweating the onions to 'drive out the moisture' and break down the cell structure, after which the onions are covered (so that they don't dry out) and stewed in their own juice. Some add salt to speed up the moisture loss, some add sugar to speed the caramelisation. Here's what I do: slice the onions as finely as possible and add to a bowl with coarse salt, then, using latex gloves if necessary, thoroughly scrunch everything together in your hands. You may weep. This is all to the good.

Now melt some butter in a big pan and drop in the onions on a medium heat. They will quickly wilt, dropping into a mush on the base of the pan. You don't want this layer to be too thick – hence the largest pan you have. Ride the heat so that the onions are cooking gently, but do not allow them to take colour. Now, this is where we get blasphemous. Add just enough water to cover the layer of onions and raise the heat enough to boil it off. Then repeat. Then repeat again. In a sense, this stands to reason. The onions are stewing in an onion-flavoured juice, just a lot faster than they might have, and the addition of the water makes it easier to prevent burning.

The clever thing about adding water during a frying process is that the oil or fat you started with floats on the surface and remains when the water boils off. Each time you boil the water completely away, the onions will be softer, and each time they'll get another touch of frying from the butter. It seems more aggressive and interventionist than long, slow stewing under a cartouche, but it works faster and better.

When you've achieved a really soft consistency, you can sprinkle on a little sugar if you wish and then start allowing the onions to 'catch' just a little in the drying pan. You don't want the onions themselves to burn, but you do want the sugary sludge to stick to the bottom of the pan and heat just enough to caramelise. What's really important to understand is that the onions are not going brown because they are burning. They are actually changing colour because you are constantly scraping caramelised sugars from where they have stuck to the bottom of the pan and dissolving them back into the onion mulch.[48] You are now as prepared as a brasserie chef with a brigade of underpaid scullions to do his onions.

To make your soup, take a ladleful of the onions and a couple of ladles of the broth per person and heat them in a saucepan. Adjust the seasoning, including, if so inclined, a glug of Worcestershire sauce and some sherry. Transfer the soup to individual ovenproof soup bowls and top with a thick disc of bread, cut as closely as possible to the size of the bowl as to form a lid. Drop this onto the top of the soup and allow it to absorb as much as it wishes. You can speed up the process by dressing the top with a drizzle more broth. Now sprinkle over a thick cap of grated Gruyère, not being too fussy about it overhanging the sides. Put the bowls onto a baking sheet and transfer to a hot oven, which, if you have suitable control over it, should have plenty of heat coming from overhead.[49]

Everybody knows that FOS is such a health and safety disaster that it should probably be banned in all responsible jurisdictions, but we shall persist. Remind your guests that the soup is only marginally cooler than molten titanium and that the melted cheese will adhere to human flesh, then sit around as food lovers have done for centuries, and make polite conversation about philosophy, poetry, art or love until it's cooled down enough to stick in your spoon.

[48] Caramel is an amazingly effective food colouring. If, for example, you want your beef broth to be a deep, mahogany brown, put a teaspoonful of sugar into a dry pan and heat it until it turns liquid and then *just* blackens. Now let it cool, then 'deglaze' the pan with a very little boiling water and a small wire whisk. The resultant liquid will dye a litre or so of stock the very deepest brown.
[49] Brown the cheese with a torch if you lack the equipment or are feeling particularly cheffy.

Valpellinentze

French onion soup is all very well in a Parisian brasserie, where all you need fortifying for is another day of strolling the boulevards, knocking out a quick painting or writing a couple of thousand words about a madeleine… again… but these don't make particularly strenuous demands upon the body. If you want a soup that's really going to set you up for the day, you need to travel to the Alpine regions of north-west Italy, where 'men are men' and soup is *valpellinentze.*

You'll need a whole savoy cabbage – because nothing much else can survive up there – from which you have removed the tough stem. You could, I suppose, go for cavolo nero or kale, but it wouldn't really be in the spirit of the thing. Render down a handful of chopped pancetta in some olive oil until you have enough fat running to ensure your survival through a bleak winter and then gently sauté the leaves in it.

Take ten or so slices of Italian bread and toast them gently in the oven until they're very crisp, then lay a couple of slices in the bottom of a broad bowl that will fit in the oven (a *cazuela* would be great).

Now, at this point you're supposed to start moistening the bread with the roasting juices of meat but, unless you've just slaughtered a superannuated milker and roasted it over a spit for the whole village, the chances are you're going to need something more akin to the beefy broth in a French onion soup (see page 162). Pour a little of this broth over the toasted bread, season very sparingly with a pinch of ground cinnamon and the merest scraping of nutmeg, then add a layer of the cabbage leaves and another of shredded pancetta.

Repeat this process, like a surrealist lasagne, until you run out of ingredients. Try to finish with a layer of cabbage and then pour in more of the broth until everything is just covered. Let everything soak for a few minutes and then top up again with the broth. It's important to make sure that everything is completely saturated. If you underestimate the amount of broth needed, you'll have to redefine your soup as a stew, and if you're really tight with it, you'll end up with a cake.

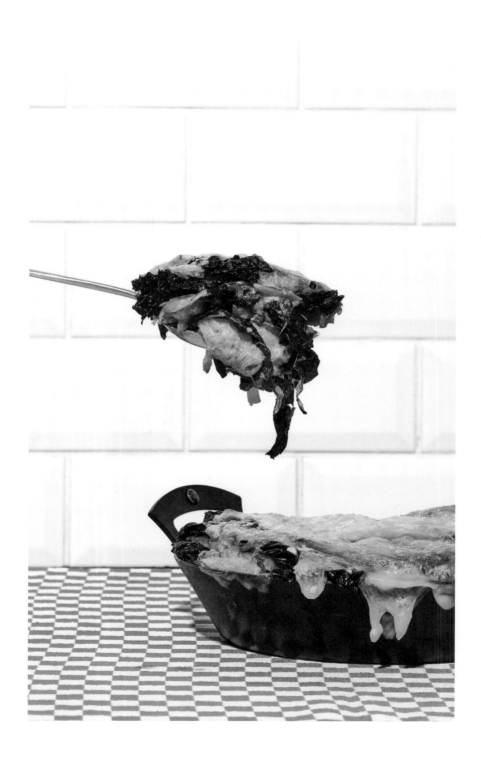

WITH & FROM BREAD

Finally, top with a thick layer of fontina cheese and place in a low oven for half an hour or so. Everything in the bowl is already cooked and, hopefully, sealed with that layer of cheese, so nothing much should evaporate while all the ingredients get to know each other by sharing a bath.

The final dish should be of such a texture that you can eat it with a spoon. You should be able to take a large helping as the first snowdrifts build up against the front door and then fall asleep in front of the fire until spring.

Bread Containers

One particularly elegant use of fried bread comes from a mash-up of a street food from Tainan called 'coffin bread' and the largely forgotten vol-au-vent, usually attributed to Marie-Antoine Carême.

Take a loaf of white bread – something with a close and regular texture – cut off the crusts and then slice the crumb into large, regular cuboids. You can make a normal-sized loaf into two main-course-sized coffins, four starter-sized or a whole undertaker's worth of canapé-sized ones.[50]

Slice a good thick 'top' off each cuboid and then use a small, sharp knife to make four cuts down into the bottom piece. Create a thick wall, at least a centimetre (just under half an inch thick) and then carefully pluck out the interior, leaving a thick bottom. Paint the box you have created, and the lid, with clarified butter on all sides and then bake, flipping the pieces around every now and again until crisp and golden, inside and out.

If you're well organised you can add your filling to the case while it's still hot, but actually, they take well to being allowed to cool on a wire rack and then quickly reheated for serving.

Fillings can be anything you fancy. Fried bread is too absorbent for anything liquid, so don't try coffins full of soup or stew, but, like vols-au-vent, they are best with thickened sauces or gravies. A full-on prawn cocktail looks great (with or without avocado), and anything bound in a cheesy béchamel works superbly, particularly if you put a little grated cheese on top and gently torch it. A coffin will hold together small ingredients, like grilled chicken livers or hearts, and if you want to go full Carême, you could even knock up a thick ragout of diced kidneys in Madeira gravy.

---

[50] The brilliant Jacques Pépin has, in his encyclopaedic books on classical technique, a recipe for a 'Pullman' loaf, where a long *pain de mie* is turned into a crust coffin and the neatly excised inside is transformed into forty or so canapé-sized sandwiches… which are then packed back into the loaf! Truly, for some great men, life is not too short.

The idea of serving soup or stew in a loaf could ordinarily be ignored as an appalling gimmick. In my home town, I remember a local entrepreneur trying to launch the 'concept' that would inevitably make him rich – hard-baked crusty rolls, hollowed out and served with a choice of fillings. There was 'chillie-con-carne' [sic], an unattributable 'stew' and some sort of chicken thing in white sauce with sweetcorn that looked like it had already been eaten once. It might have been less abominable if he'd thought to serve them at a table, but he felt that, as his target competition – McDonalds, Burger King and Wimpy – served food to be consumed on the move, this was how he was going to crack into the big markets and make his billions.

You will have noticed the main technical issue here – that of walking along the promenade of an evening with a bowl of boiling slop and then, basically, biting the side out of the bowl. I think he lasted about six weeks before the last customer finally disappeared, disheartened by a scalded chin or a huge dry-cleaning bill.

Bunny Chow

There are, however, a couple of foods for which the loaf makes sense as a container. Bunny chow originated in Durban, but has since become a de facto national dish of South Africa, perhaps because the many myths surrounding it are all rooted in the country's apartheid history, and bunny chow is one of the vanishingly tiny number of good things that came out of that period. Bunny chow consists of a white loaf, cut in half, hollowed out and filled with curry. The name is probably derived from '*bania*', the caste of Indian restaurant owners who served it out of the back of the kitchen to black workers who were barred from the main restaurant. The bread itself is the standard 'tin loaf' that spread wherever the British colonised and meant that nobody need be troubled with crockery or cutlery.

A 'bunny' can be eaten on the move using fingers and the lid of the loaf as a spoon. The last remains of the sauce soak into the bread container, which is then torn apart and consumed. I'm trying hard to think of anything in the English repertoire with that many cultural resonances, and if South Africans proudly enjoy their curry out of a loaf, I'm not going to be the one to belittle it as a gimmick.

In fact, let's not have a recipe for bunny chow. Let's get an extra helping of something good next time we're having a takeaway, let's serve it straight into a hollowed-out loaf and eat it with our fingers, and let's think about what thoroughly delicious things come out of human ingenuity in the face of adversity.

Cioppino

In the States, the hollowed-out loaf is a popular tourist food that, for some reason, has become associated with seaports. In San Francisco, *cioppino* – an Italian fish stew – is served in a hollowed boule of sourdough, and along the north-eastern coast it's creamy clam or fish chowder. I worked in restaurants in both places and, even as a careless youth, it troubled me that the bread was never eaten. Loaf after loaf came back to the wash-up, to be scraped straight into the bin.

It was a time and a culture less troubled by kitchen waste than we are today, but that wasn't what got me. My greed told me that these bloody idiots were just chucking out the best bit and it completely infuriated me. Today, whenever I travel to either coast, I'll still order the *cioppino* or the chowder, if only out of gastronomic nostalgia, as it's just too easy to ask for the whole thing to be brought to you in a bowl.

After the first bits are eaten with spoon and fork, you can start ripping the bread apart, and yes, particularly in posher places, they'll look at you like you're dismembering a live poodle, but you know the truth. They're the fools, and you're eating the best bits.

There are plenty of recipes for chowders on the Internet and you can find good clams and mussels in the freezer section of the supermarket now, in sealed pouches with all the vital juices that make for good broth. Next to them, though, you'll also find frozen lobsters that are remarkably cheap and often marked down in price as their sell-by dates approach. I usually buy them up when they hit 'two for a fiver'.

Frozen lobsters seem to come in gluts. I understand they're boiled and frozen on big boats, and I'm sure they're not the right thing for a lobster salad or something elegant. They are great, though, for pasta sauces, soups, lobster rolls and, in this particular case, kind of 'chowdery' stews.

Defrost the lobsters and pick out their meat, being careful to catch any juices, odd bits or weirdly unrecognisable pasty materials. Put the meat to one side and put the shells and everything else in an oven tray, breaking up the big pieces. Roast everything in the tray until you start to get a little bit of scorching on the edges.

In a big pot, sweat some onions and a chopped stick of celery until they're translucent. Now add a tablespoon of tomato purée and cook until it loses its acidic edge. Pour in the contents of the baking tray and, while it's still hot, rinse out the bottom of it with vermouth, taking care to scrape vigorously to dissolve any stuck-on and browned material. Pour some white wine into the big pot and cook off the alcohol, then add a couple of pints of milk and bring to just below a simmer.

Slice the top off a boule loaf – the supermarket ones are excellent for this – and tear out the inner crumb. Paint the inside of the loaf and the lid with melted butter. Cut the crumb into regular cubes and fry in clarified butter to make golden-brown croutons. Set to one side.

Peel a few potatoes, cut them into cubes, then fry them a little in the buttery frying pan along with some chopped whites of leeks. Strain the milky lobster stock through a sieve into the frying pan, pushing down hard on the detritus to extract every last bit of flavour. Put the loaf into the hot oven to just faintly brown on the inside.

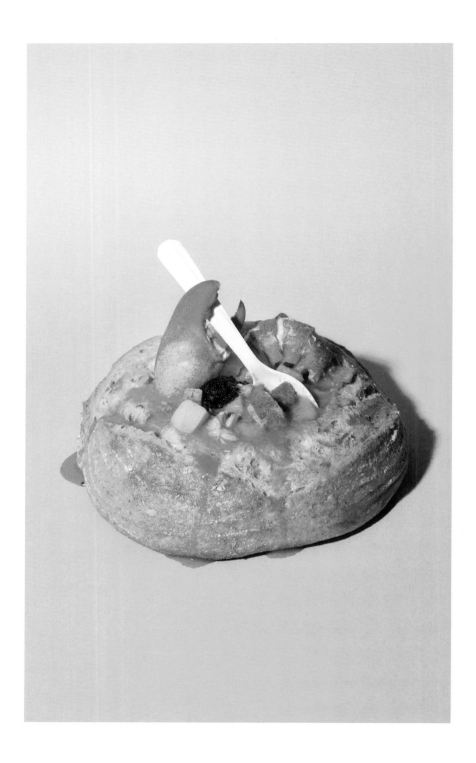

Once the potato cubes have cooked through to softness, stir through some cream and the lobster meat.

Adjust the seasoning with salt, black pepper and a small squirt of sriracha, then pour into the loaf, topping with the croutons and a couple of teaspoonfuls of cheap lumpfish or Japanese salmon roe – which you will casually refer to as 'caviar' when serving.

It's not a bisque, and it's not really a chowder either, but it's as luxurious as all hell. It looks absurdly impressive served in a loaf and the best thing is that nobody will *dare* to leave the bread uneaten.

WITH & FROM BREAD

The Majesty of Bread and Chicken

There are meals that stick in your memory forever, and I've been lucky enough to have had many. The really good ones change the way you think about an ingredient or dish for all time, and for me the most memorable of these was a simple roast chicken at Zuni Café in San Francisco.

Ask most food lovers about the Zuni chicken and they'll talk about the brining. Chef Judy Rodgers was one of the first to publicise the idea of salting the bird a day or two ahead of cooking to enhance the flavour – and it was, indeed, a boon to humanity worthy of a Nobel Prize for Roasting – but what had me near to tears at the table was the bread salad that accompanied the roast bird.

It was rough-torn chunks of rustic white bread, a few crusts left for texture, grilled, dressed in roasting juices, olive oil and carefully curated vinegars, and all served over bitter frisée shot through with soaked raisins and roasted pine nuts. It was, not to put too fine a point on it, stellar – and, quite apart from the whole stunning experience of the meal, it cemented in my mind forever the relationship between roast chicken and simple white bread.

Top in the category of 'things that shouldn't be so damn good but really are' is a supermarket rotisserie chicken, shredded into a supermarket baked baguette, with just a thick smear of butter and a few crystals of sea salt. With the bread warm and the chicken almost too hot to rip into, the butter sinks into the loaf in a manner that's almost troublingly erotic. So completely seducing is it that I've been known to construct one of these in the car park.

The combination works in many iterations. Sliced chicken breast on sliced white is a lovely thing. Simple, pure and with the only question to trouble the mind being whether a smear of mayonnaise is better than thick butter, salt and black pepper – there's something about the combination that gets you into these Jesuitical refinements. Skin on/skin off? Darker meat, torn from thighs? The oysters dug from just above the hipbones, confited in their own fat and pan juice… perhaps a denser, slightly sweeter white bread? Definitely lots of salty butter this time… mayo would be too much… the salt cuts the fat.

It never gets old, either. I'll come back to the chicken sandwich as I sit on the edge of my bunk waiting for the prison chaplain to lead me out, and I refine and improve the chicken and bread salad combo every time I cook it – at time of writing, about once a month. The first way I strayed from Rodgers' true path was to combine the raisins, pine nuts and torn bread, soak them in a little water and stuff them into the chicken. The water steams the chicken from within, and the bread, in exchange, soaks up even more of the chicken's fat and juices. I roast the bird, initially, in the usual way – slowly and lying in two positions, first on its breast, then, as the core temperature begins to rise close to finished, flipped breast-up and the stuffing pulled out into a separate roasting pan. It still has the power to absorb a good sprinkling of oil or maybe some dots of butter, but then it goes back in alongside the chicken so that they can both crisp and tan.

The roasted bread-stuffing salad is rich, so bitter leaves and lemon juice or vinegar are still the ideal foil, but this is not yet the ultimate iteration. The chicken and bread salad is supreme for a glorious summer lunch, but for a winter evening we need something more… using the bread to unite the ideas of roast chicken and French onion soup.

We are still in awed homage to Judy Rodgers, so the night before you plan to cook, salt your chicken vigorously, inside and out, and tear a white loaf into big chunks. Leave the bread out to stale, and cover the chicken loosely and put it in the fridge.

Clarify and caramelise half a dozen big white onions (see page 162)[51]. When you're ready to roast, pack a layer of stale bread chunks into a baking tray, top with a thin layer of the caramelised onions and then a generous grating of Gruyère. Construct a second layer of bread on top, then pour over chicken stock until you can see it pooling between the chunks.

[51] You can also do this overnight in a slow cooker if you have one.

Wait a little to ensure that the bread is soaking up the stock, then top up with a little more and now…. well, now we should pause for dramatic effect…

…because the next step is to place the chicken on top of everything. Yep, just perch it there like the *Rokeby Venus*, recumbent on a damp duvet.

Season the top of the bird as you usually would and then gently slide the entire teetering edifice into the oven. Cooking time will depend on the size of your chicken, but 75°C (167°F) internal temperature at the thigh joint is safe.

Once cooked, remove the chicken and pour any juices from the cavity into the bread, which by now will have puffed up like something halfway between *The Blob* (1958) and some sort of swamp soufflé. Crank the oven to full, and while the chicken rests on the table, slide the bread base back in. Ferociously brown the top of the bastard.

I like to serve the chicken on top of the bread. It makes an absurd visual impact placed in the centre of the table, and any juices released as you dismember the bird will just enrich the bread. You can serve the bread with a big spoon, making sure you include some crispy bits, some soft and spongy stuff, a good portion of the sweetened onions and great twangy strings of the melted Gruyère with each helping.

You'll still need the bitter leaves and you'll almost certainly want any dressing to be tart – hell, you're probably going to want a medic on standby with a defibrillator – but, like that very first chicken I ate at Zuni Café, I can guarantee you'll never forget it.

Bread (and Butter) Pudding

There is a name for the kind of hot/wet bread we saw in the wintery Zuni chicken with bread strata – in classical French cookery, it's called a *panade*. It's rarely associated with refined dishes and it's not seen that often in British savoury cooking – perhaps we can't quite handle any more dampness – but it does appear in some characteristically British desserts. Bread pudding is, effectively, a sweetened *panade*. It works well made with brown bread, where the malty, nutty notes combine with the caramelising sugars to make something that just cries out for custard.

Some people like bread and butter pudding to be made thin, in a wide pan, so that it can be cut into delicate slivers and served politely. It's made with a lot of eggs and they proudly speak of its resemblance to a poncey French *pain perdu*. They lay out the slices of bread in neat and pleasing patterns or, and I apologise for this, they make it from panettone.

For me, this is not in the spirit of a 'pudding' – which, in its earliest and most beloved forms, was effectively a lump of boiled suet dough. A bread pudding should be made deep, even in a loaf tin, and carved into big, rude lumps or spooned out like Stilton from a truckle.

Lavishly butter slices of malty brown bread, tear them into large pieces and stick them around the bottom and sides of a regular loaf tin. You could butter the tin first, but if you're being generous enough in smearing your bread, this won't be necessary. Be aware that this is one of the most important parts of the process, for it is these slices that will *fry* in this butter when the pan hits the hot oven. This is the key element – the chief characteristic of a good bread and butter pudding. It's why we tear the slices before we stick them in… because torn edges catch and brown.

Tear up the rest of the bread and soak it in lots of milk. After ten minutes or so you'll be able to beat it like a thick batter, into which you'll be able to stir demerara sugar, a couple of eggs, some melted butter and loads of raisins or sultanas that you've soaked for half an hour in hot tea. Season unreasonably with cinnamon and nutmeg.

Your finished mix should look, as my grandfather averred, like M10 grade concrete,[52] but only barely pourable. Scrape it into your bread-and-butter-lined tin, bang it on the work surface to make sure there are no air pockets that might compromise its set strength and then top with a thick crust of more demerara sugar. Bake for ninety minutes before cranking up the oven to crisp the top and make everything golden.

Serve warm with clotted cream, ice cream, custard or any combination thereof, but, as a sufficiently fruity bread pudding is consanguineous with dark fruit cakes, you'll find it's even better cut into a large slice, wrapped in greaseproof paper and hiked with to somewhere miles from prying eyes, where it can be properly enjoyed.

Bread 'Pond' Pudding

If you'd prefer to make something a little more appropriate to a dinner party than the noble bread pudding – and, who knows, there may be people reading this who would – then it's possible to mash up the bread pudding with the infinitely more middle-class Sussex pond pudding, veteran of a thousand '70s restaurants and countless *Abigail's Parties*.

The impossibly racy premise of the Sussex pond pudding that so enchanted post-war Britain was a whole, exotic lemon, packed in sugar and butter into a capsule of suet pastry and steamed until it collapsed into what would doubtless have been described as an 'indulgent' treat. It's not that difficult to knock up and, yes, it does make an impressive display when cut into at table – but it can be punishingly sweet or face-shrivellingly tart if you don't get the balance right, and, if you've failed to cook it for long enough, chewing the skin is less than pleasurable.

Instead, line a small metal pudding basin with a layer of dense white bread, cut into slices, crusts removed and very generously buttered on both sides. Make sure all gaps are filled. Now add another bread layer, also well

[52] 1:3:6 ratio of cement/sand/aggregate. Compressive strength of 10 MPa.

buttered, trying to ensure that the joins in the first layer are covered by the slices in the second.

Use a clean tea towel or J Cloth soaked in vodka to wash the outside of a small orange. A navel would be good when in season, a blood orange will cause your guests to swoon at your brilliance and a Seville will win you extra points for 'a sophisticated balance of sour and bitter in the flavour profile'. This might also work nicely with a satsuma or clementine, but since the supermarkets renamed them 'easy peelers', I recommend we should boycott them altogether.

Over a baking tray, vigorously exfoliate the skin of your fruit with a handful of demerara sugar. Make sure not to lose a single crystal of it because it will have absorbed a great deal of fragrant oil as well as rendering the skin more porous. Drop the whole orange into your bread-lined pudding bowl, pack cubes of salted butter (yes, salted) into any crevices, then pour over the exfoliating rub and some extra sugar for luck.[53]

Try to ensure that your packing brings the filling of the pudding right up to the rim of the basin, then apply a thick bread lid, also buttered on both sides, and wrap the whole arrangement tightly with cling film.[54]

Take a large pan with a well-fitting lid and screw up a tea towel in the bottom of it. Place the wrapped pudding on the cloth, then pour in water until it comes nearly to the top of the pudding basin. Put the pot over a low heat and allow to just simmer, with the lid on, for three to four hours, topping up with water from a boiled kettle if necessary.

Take the pudding out. Depending on your timings, you can now leave it to stand until you're nearly ready to serve or you can plough straight on. Turn up the oven to its highest heat. Unwrap the pudding and cover the

---

[53] Estimate the size of both the orange and the bowl so that there is only the smallest amount of wriggle room between orange and bread. You'll fill any space with sugar and butter, but too much of that stuff will clog your arteries.
[54] Top Chef Tip. As long as it doesn't touch the hot surface of the oven or an open flame, cling film is effectively ovenproof. Many commercial chefs will wrap a roast in cling film and then foil before a long, slow roasting, only removing them after the meat has rested for a final ferocious browning… much like this pudding.

top with a piece of foil, buttered on the inside and cinched tight over the top of the bowl. Put the whole pudding on a baking sheet to catch any overspill and put into the oven for ten minutes.

The buttered bread layers will have kept the ingredients together as well as suet pastry, though with less of the texture of an armoured tyre. The fruit will have collapsed, and the liquid elements of the filling will have combined. The cling film will have held everything in place and the quick final burst of heat will fry the buttered bread exterior and caramelise any leaks.

If you're planning to turn the pudding out at the table, loosen it first in the privacy of the kitchen. It will save massive embarrassment. As it's hotter than lava when it comes out of the oven, you could even transfer it to a cold pudding basin of similar size, discreetly lubricated with a little more butter. It should pop out at the table like a greased frog, to admiring gasps from your guests.

Bread Sauce

The purest *panade* is probably the very British phenomenon of bread sauce, which is served with game birds and Christmas dinner, but really should be available with every meal in a special silver pot at the centre of the table. At its simplest, it's hot milk into which fresh white breadcrumbs are stirred, breaking down to create a pure, smooth paste. There's an argument that this should be enough to provide a foil to properly high-hung game with a rich, dark gravy but, thank goodness, most cooks can't leave well alone.

Bread sauce usually begins with ingredients infused into the milk. It's traditional to start with a bay leaf and large, peeled onion stuck with a couple of cloves. Personally, I can take or leave bay, and I think cloves taste like one of Starbucks' 'seasonal' slurries. The onion is a great thing, so I will keep that, but if I'm going to add a spice it might just be a pod or two of cardamom.

Once the milk has taken on the flavours you want, strain it to remove any solids. Toss the spices, but you might want to consider keeping the onion.

Add the bread a little at a time or the sauce will take on a life of its own and, like some invasive alien life form, grow to a terrifying size. Keeping the milk at less than a simmer, add a small handful of breadcrumbs and observe their behaviour. First they sit, soaking, then they sink, and any larger pieces quietly get bigger as they absorb and then break up… and then absorb more. If you add too much, you'll end up topping up with liquid…then adding more crumbs, then more liquid…

Heat everything really slowly, stirring constantly and carefully. There is a short window between achieving the perfect consistency and scorching the bottom of the pan.[55]

As soon as you feel you have it right, take the sauce off the heat and consider your options. You should obviously season – plenty of salt and ground white pepper[56] – but, aside from a couple of hundred years of sclerotic tradition, there's nothing stopping you taking things further. Cream is an obvious improver. You could add cheese. Yes, cheese. A scrape of Parmesan or a big old handful of Gruyère will transform the sauce completely. Yes, it's closer to a mornay sauce, but who's going to sue us? But what's going to blow the minds of traditionalists is when you take that poached onion you saved, chop it into the sauce and then clobber it smooth with an immersion blender. 'It's a *soubise*!' they will whinge. 'Bollocks,' you will reply. 'It's much better.'

[55] About the same amount of time it takes light to travel one Planck length.
[56] White pepper was classified as a fully Mortal Sin at some point around 1980. Chefs are trained to use white pepper in white sauces so that there are no ugly black flecks, but everybody is missing the point here. White pepper tastes different from black. It has a complicated fragrance with elements of mace and nutmeg… both of which you'd probably want to add separately if you used black pepper.

Passatelli

There are recipes in every food culture that are about using up leftovers and elevating thrift to an art form, but it took the Italians to codify it into *cucina povera*, or 'poverty cooking' – folk recipes, mostly from rural Central Italy, which combine the validation of thrift with the pleasure of great flavours. *Passatelli* is a 'pasta' that perfectly expresses the idea. It begins with stale white bread, grated finely and regularly, which is combined with grated Parmesan and bound with egg. Toothless little old grannies in rural Emilia-Romagna will recall making it after the war with kilos of iron-hard bread, the tiniest scrapings from a carefully hoarded Parmesan rind and an egg that had been bartered for two days' labour on a road-making gang. Water would have made up for any lack of moisture. Recipes today suggest a relatively abstemious 1:1 ratio of bread to cheese, bound with one egg to each 150g (5oz) of dry ingredients, but slyly mention that wealthier families 'might have used more cheese'.

The dough is rested and then pushed through a purpose-built press, which extrudes it into thick little rods. You can use a potato ricer or *spätzle* maker to get the same effect. Perhaps the most satisfying way, though, is to feed the dough into a mincer fitted with a coarse plate and the star-shaped 'cutter' removed. The resulting fat noodles/long gnocchi/dumpling sticks can be dropped straight into a well-flavoured chicken broth, where they'll poach and quickly cook through – they float when they're done.

You can eat them just like that, *in brodo*, or you can lift them out and serve them with grated cheese. Because there's less free gluten in *passatelli* than there would be in pasta, long strands will not survive cooking in one piece, so it's best to cut both your losses and the pasta into short lengths.

Crab Cakes

Pure crabmeat can be finely ground until almost puréed, shaped into a patty and fried, but doing this produces a solid lump of homogenous protein – the kind of fishcake or ball that you might find in Chinese or Thai cookery. The American crab cake, however, is more lightly textured and crucially 'stretches' the strong flavour of the meat into something much more filling.

It might seem odd to think of a crab cake as a bread recipe but, ultimately, bread is the main bulk of the dish. You can strip your own fresh crab if you're keen, but in truth this works extremely well with tinned or frozen crab, or the stuff that supermarkets now sell sealed in plastic pods. Separate the brown from the white meat and try to keep as many large chunks intact as you can.

Stir the brown meat into a similar quantity of mayonnaise – I favour the Japanese Kewpie mayo because it has much more of an umami element – and then add the same amount of breadcrumbs as the combined brown meat and mayo.

Finally, add the flaky white meat and delicately fork it through. No need to combine too thoroughly, as the idea is to keep things light. For the same reason, don't over-handle the mixture to make neat patties or, God forbid, force it into a cheffy quenelle or a ring – just dollop a spoonful into a hot pan with some clarified butter and then when it's time to flip, squish it lightly and bring up the sides into a rough patty shape.

It's no wonder that the crab cake is a restaurateur's favourite. The expensive ingredients add all sorts of punchy flavours, but it's the stale bread *panade* that's carrying the dish, soaking up all the goodness and crisping in the hot butter, yet steaming and soft within.

Meatloaf

Stretching ingredients with breadcrumbs isn't just a matter of adding filler, like gravel in concrete. The important thing about bread, particularly the stale stuff, is its ability to suck up moisture and hold it. It's particularly good at holding in fat, which adds huge amounts of flavour but would otherwise separate.

If you've ever been subjected to a well-meaning cook's first attempts at home sausage making, you'll have had first-hand experience of this. The first thing most sausage makers want to do is 'get rid of all those awful commercial fillers' that you find in butcher's sausages. They buy premium meat, season it well, grind it smooth and pipe it into skins… which then make the most appalling sausages. Heavy, dull, with a rubbery texture and none of the life-affirming joy of a proper banger.

Butcher's sausages are made with a quantity of 'rusk'. This is a simple white bread that's been baked twice[57] before being ground to a carefully measured granularity. You can make your own by chucking some dry toast in the blender. But here's the key point: a good sausage is, indeed, made from meat that might otherwise not be used, or has a challenging texture, but the butcher knows that that is where all the flavour lies – there, and in the fat.

The meat is ground to make it more palatable, the fat supplies more flavour, unctuousness, lubrication and juiciness, and the rusk – the vital rusk – holds the fat inside the mixture. It soaks up the fats and juices and holds them. The sausage is a triumph of the butcher's skill in selecting and re-texturising some of their best products, and it's rusk that makes it all possible.

I *could* tell you that you can do the same thing with hamburger meat, and create an absolutely astonishingly good burger by using 'fillers' to ensure that all that delicious beefy fat and juice doesn't leak straight out of the burger, to evaporate in a heartbreakingly pointless puff of steam on the carefully sourced hickory logs below. I could tell you that, but you'd laugh

---

[57] *Bis cuit* if you want to go all haute cuisine about it.

and say, 'Nobody's put breadcrumbs in a hamburger since Fanny Cradock', and then a gang of tattooed blokes with huge beards, wearing leather aprons would drag me into the street to 're-educate' me for my breach of doctrine.

I discovered one of my favourite pieces of unintentional food writing when I was still too skinny to know what a decent meal was. Tucked in my backpack, like every other callow oaf with literary ambitions, was a copy of Jack Kerouac's *The Dharma Bums*. Before spending sixty-three days alone in a fire-watcher's lookout post on Desolation Peak, The Traveller stocks up on burgers from a roadside joint. Dozens of them, wrapped tightly in greaseproof paper and jammed into the bottom of his backpack.

I loved that piece of writing. I grew out of Kerouac pretty quickly, as we all did – his self-obsessed adolescent proto-hippy Zen 'philosophy' was never going to survive contact with the adult world and could be safely ignored – but he knew even then, as I know now, that food from roadside shacks is good, in spite of itself, and that a good burger is good cold – and I'm damned sure his had more than a handful of filler in them.

Maybe the world isn't ready to welcome back *panade* in a burger, but there's another dish in the American canon, rare in the UK, that uses the principle to brilliant effect: meatloaf.

There are as many recipes for meatloaf as there are hassled 'moms' stretching their budgets in the US, but when you know the principles, it's fairly easy to make up your own. You'll need beef mince and pork mince as your base – beef by itself is boring and not fatty enough – along with a beaten egg to hold things together and some fresh breadcrumbs. Most written recipes you'll find for meatloaf try to make it more luxurious, indulgent and, frankly, modern, by reducing the quantity of breadcrumbs and going for better cuts of meat. This is equivalent to whatever the philosophical opposite of a false economy is; it's more expensive *and* it doesn't taste as good.

You can now go to town on the seasoning – but not just in the ordinary way, sprinkling in dry stuff like herbs and mustard powder or little touches of damp stuff like Worcestershire or Tabasco sauce. You have Secret Knowledge. You know the awesome absorbative power of your breadcrumbs, so you can glug in Marsala, blob in a load of ketchup or mayo, or smooth things out with cream cheese, double cream or yoghurt. If you like, you can add *more* breadcrumbs to soak up *more* amazingness.

Drop the combined mixture into a greased loaf tin, cover with foil and cook until a probe thermometer reads 75°C (167°F) at the centre.[58] Allow to rest in the tin to reabsorb any absconding juices, then serve in thick, juicy slices as you consider this thought: meatloaf, that much derided proletarian treat, without its bread and the delights that bread is able to retain, would be merely a posh terrine… and where's the fun in that?

Croquetas

When soaked for a while, breadcrumbs lose their form and become a relatively smooth starch paste.[59] With the judicious application of an immersion blender, this can be entirely smooth. This is, in every respect, identical to a béchamel or white roux, only a lot less fuss to knock up.

We'll use this miraculous quality elsewhere in the book, too, but for now, it's enough to know that you can use it to make absolutely stunning Spanish *croquetas* – and with about half the faff of the usual method, thereby removing the only reason that might stop you eating them at every single meal until you die.

---

[58] I do not presume to suggest the size or shape of your tin. This works beautifully as a 'loaf' but is no bad thing as a shallower 'cake'… though obviously 'meat cake' has less immediate appeal on a menu.
[59] Technically a starch gel (see page 142).

Bring some milk to just below a simmer and pour in a handful of white or panko breadcrumbs.[60] Allow them to soak for a while and then, if things remain liquid, add another handful. Keep going until you reach the consistency of a really thick custard. Now ply the immersion blender. This will thicken the sauce further, meaning that you'll be granted the tremendous opportunity to loosen it with butter and cream. Add salt and taste regularly while you adjust the flavour and texture.

Next beat in your flavouring element. Chopped *jamón* or grated Spanish cheese would be traditional, some tinned or fresh crabmeat would be a luxury, lobster meat beyond wild dreams and probably illegal in several administrations.

Allow the flavoured mixture to cool, then take a spoonful at a time and shape into spheres or cylinders before returning to the fridge to set.

You can roll the *croquetas* in egg wash and breadcrumbs before frying or just in a coat of seasoned flour. Either way, they'll crisp beautifully as they enter the deep-fat fryer, while the filling will warm through and return to a positively indecent consistency that actually *spurts* when bitten.

---

[60] Panko can be substituted for white breadcrumbs in any recipe – they are similarly without pronounced flavour – but just remember they'll absorb almost twice as much liquid.

Skordalia

Using *panade* to absorb liquids and flavours gives us one of the most subtle recipes, in bread sauce, and one of the most ferocious – and they are closely related.

Skordalia is a Greek dip or sauce that often comes as a meze, or can be offered as a sort of relish alongside roast meats. It's not unrelated to *aioli* or the other garlic-based suspensions, but it's thickened and stabilised with bread. You're supposed to do all this in a pestle and mortar for peasant authenticity, but honestly, who has the time – and though I don't know any Greek peasants personally, I'd be prepared to make a substantial cash bet that if you offered them a blender, they'd embrace it with enthusiasm and gladness.

Crush a few garlic cloves first. It's possible to use garlic by itself as an emulsifying agent, as anyone who has made allioli with just a clove of garlic, olive oil, a knife and plate will readily attest.[61]

Tear white bread into small pieces, throwing away the crusts, and beat them into the smashed garlic to form a paste. Season with salt, pepper and a little lemon juice, then start adding the olive oil drop by drop. The sauce should begin to 'mount' like a mayonnaise, though with a slightly less opaque, creamy colour. Balance the flavours with a little vinegar and lemon juice, and that's it. Some recipes pound in walnuts or almonds, somewhat in the manner of a pesto, but the main point of the *skordalia* is usually the garlic, raw and fiery.

It is possible, though, to rebalance the ingredients in a traditional *skordalia* to make an incredibly smooth and luxurious dip that's a subtle and elegant alternative to hummus. Begin by poaching a clove or two of garlic in a small amount of milk. Remove the garlic, then add crushed almonds and white breadcrumbs to the pan and stir on a low heat. It's important for the finished result that you can actually distinguish the

---

[61] Actually, I'm not sure I've ever met anyone who can do this. It's supposed to be possible – in fact, it's often issued as a challenge to non-Spaniards – but I've yet to witness it.

taste of the bread, so it's worth using a fresh Italian loaf or a baguette. Sourdough is a little too strident. Use a blender to ensure the paste is completely free of lumps, then add a well-flavoured olive oil in a thin stream until you have the texture of a smooth parfait. A little salt and lemon juice will finish it off, but it's important to taste as you season. You must be able to clearly distinguish the fragrance of the oil, plus the almonds and, most importantly, the bread.

Just when you think you've entirely exhausted the shape-shifting possibilities of soaked bread, there's one last thing to consider. When left to go cold, *panade* will go solid. It's a similar effect to chilling polenta. This means it can be sliced into pieces that can be toasted or fried. There is something pleasingly circular about taking slices of bread, staling, drying and crumbling them, turning them into a smooth white sauce, and then chilling, setting and slicing it and treating it exactly like a slice of bread again.

A slice of chilled, highly flavoured bread sauce, dredged in seasoned flour, then fried in clarified butter, is the perfect thing to slip under something dark and gamey. Or you can do it with a very plain version to support a more delicate topping, such as a slice of smoked eel or mackerel with *chrain* or perhaps some devilled crab (see page 205).

Dipping Bread

There's a whole class of bread use that we can usefully categorise as 'dipping' – or 'dunking', if you prefer. The absorbent quality of bread makes it an ideal eating utensil, the way it can be torn into convenient-sized chunks meaning it can completely replace a fork or spoon altogether. With a bowl of soup or stew and a small loaf (and without a disapproving audience) you can make short work of dinner, and it's entirely debatable whether you need to do any washing-up afterwards.

Dipping isn't always necessarily barbarian. Let's consider what, at least to British children, is often the first excursion into self-feeding beyond just cramming bits in: the boiled egg and soldiers. It's a combination that has occupied kids' messy attentions for centuries and which still secretly pleases most of us as adults. It's difficult to pin down exactly why it feels so good to dip bread in things. If I'd spent more money on therapy, I'd probably be able to posit that it was something to do with oral fixation, but there certainly is something about harking back to innocence. We got dippy bits of bread when we were still too young to be trusted with eating utensils. We were encouraged by loving, warm, all-providing parents to messily shovel our food into our mouths and, when we'd finished, they tenderly washed our greasy little faces. There's got to be something about that, buried in the lizard brain, that delights even the most uptight of adults.

Fondues and Melted Cheese

At the bleakest times, it is often difficult to retain faith in humanity, but then we remember that every food culture that has discovered cheese has found a way to melt it and use it for dipping bread into. It has not once been elevated to anything like haute cuisine, and yet everywhere it turns up, the Melty Cheese Product™ delights, survives and persists.

The most famous incarnation of the dippy cheese is probably Swiss fondue, which may have one or two authentic roots in Alpine villages but was mainly reinvented and introduced worldwide by the Schweizerische Käseunion, a shadowy cartel that controlled all cheese production in Switzerland. In the years following the First World War, they campaigned to have fondue declared their national dish. They created competing 'regional' recipes for the various cantons and, in the 1930s, began an aggressive campaign of promotion and advertisement. This was partly what they described as a 'spiritual defence' of Swiss nationality... but mainly because fondue used such a colossal amount of cheese.

In 1964 fondue was a popular novelty at the New York World's Fair, and it quickly became a global success story. Quite how a vast vat of boiling, indigestible cheese managed to be seen as 'sexy' is still a bit of a mystery. It may have been something to do with ads involving athletic-looking young people feeding each other with long forks or the whole 'dipping and sharing' concept somehow tapping into ideas of European sexual liberalism. Whatever it was, it was certainly nothing to do with stomach cramps, cheese sweats and catastrophic intestinal wind.

The Schweizerische Käseunion stayed firmly in control of their global expansion plans. When the US market was challenged by a widespread cultural aversion to 'double dipping', they 'discovered', as if by magic, a long-forgotten tradition that the fork was only to be used to transfer dipped food to your plate and never to be eaten from.

It is unfortunate, though perhaps not entirely surprising, that the Käseunion folded in 1999 in a corruption scandal – but their work was done. Fondue had gone global, Swiss cultural dominance was assured forever and the brilliant minds behind it have faded into obscurity... that is unless, in a hardened concrete bunker, deep in the Alps, a criminal mastermind still lurks... Dr von Due, wearing an eyepatch, stroking a cat... and waving a long fork as he lowers inconvenient spies into a vat of boiling cheese.

Much of the mythology around preparing fondue comprises quite sensible efforts to stop the cheese splitting into oil and solids or coagulating into a terrifying lump. In Mexico, *queso fundido* is the dipper's choice. Like fondue, it gets round the problems of splitting and texture by

WITH & FROM BREAD

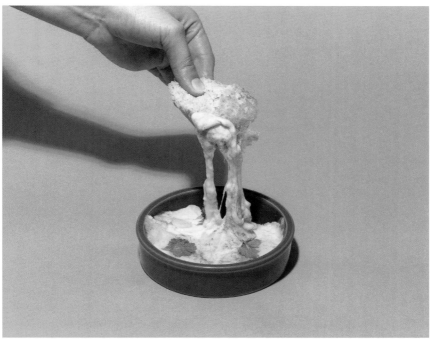

combining various types of cheese. Asadero, Manchego and Chihuahua (or *menonita*) cheeses cover all the bases of strong flavour, stringiness, meltability and stability. Asadero is close in structure and behaviour to mozzarella and Chihuahua shares some of the characteristics of Cheddar. Mexican Manchego is made from cow's milk, rather than the sheep's milk of its Spanish cousin, but a properly aged one is perhaps halfway between a mature Cheddar and a mild Parmesan. These are usually grated together and either heated in a small pan or dumped straight onto a hot griddle and then scraped up to be served. It's best spooned onto fresh, warm tortillas.

Fonduta is an Italian version of fondue, originating just over the peaks from Switzerland, but it gets round the problems of splitting and clumping in a different way. It starts with fontina, a semi-soft cheese, but combines it with egg yolks, flour, milk and butter. It has elements of béchamel, a touch of custardiness and, crucially, the sauce-like recipe makes the cheese stable. It also somehow manages to be more refined than fondue, more digestible and all-round more elegant.[62]

Some cheeses, though, are great at melting all by themselves. Camembert is already pretty soft and is contained in a physically strong rind. It requires only a little heat to become a perfect dipping medium all of its own.

Most of the French washed-rind soft cheeses have a long and distinguished pedigree as high-status delicacies. For centuries, Camembert was carefully ripened and then brought to the table to be ceremonially opened and consumed. It was only with the arrival of smaller cheeses, made for the mass market and packaged in wooden boxes for ease of delivery, that recipes began to appear for the sacrilegious act of 'baking' a Camembert.

It's a recipe that writes itself. You don't need an expensive cheese to do it – a supermarket one, reduced in price due to those who get squeamish about sell-by dates, is absolutely the best. Just open the box, pull off the wax paper, replace it with aluminium foil and put the cheese back in.

---

[62] It is also an absolutely superb substitute for the béchamel in a lasagne, elevating it – almost – to the status of a *vincisgrassi*. This fact should be kept secret from everyone except you and me. Honestly, it's so rich that if they find out, they'll take it away from us.

Pierce the top and poke in shards of garlic, a herb or two and a shot of booze, close everything up and heat it in the oven. Too simple for words and, pleasingly, evolved from the democratisation of a product and a development of modern packaging.

If you want to get classy, they now make ceramic pots that fit standard-sized cheeses. You can go even more premium with a Tunworth, a Vacherin or even an Époisses, but most important of all is that you're going to need a lot of bread. It is entirely coincidental that baguette is the best bread for this. It's not what it was designed for and there's no tradition attached to what is, effectively, a modern dish. Melted cheese, though, has a particularly gluey consistency, so unless you want to go the fondue route of staled bread cubes on long forks, you need something that has a supporting crust attached to every small piece. Rip a bit off the end of a baguette, then tear that apart and you are automatically left with the ideal dipping tool, crumb and crust in perfect ratio, with the structural integrity and the shape to scoop gloop.

Hot, Spiced Crab

Lots of things got devilled in the past: kidneys, eggs, sprats, fish roes, haddock… in fact, you could be forgiven for thinking that the Edwardians were so idiotically squeamish that they'd devil anything that had the faintest chance of smelling 'off'. It's no coincidence, then, that they devilled crab with abandon. Though it's delicious by itself, crab is also a terrific ingredient to use with pronounced seasoning, because if you use plenty of the brown meat, its flavour is strong enough to stand up to anything. If you don't like the brown meat in a crab, then a) don't bother devilling the white meat alone (it's a waste) and b) try devilled crab because it balances out the brown meat in a way you will probably find delightful.

This particular way of eating crab evolved after a trip to Lisbon. I remember little of it due to some fairly heroic drinking, save for a visit to a beautiful restaurant overlooking water somewhere that seemed to have

John Malkovich in it. I recognised crab on the menu, through the haze, and persisted in ordering it, in spite of the wise and incredibly handsome young waiter who tried to warn me that it may not be the best choice for me. What arrived was a vast spider crab, on its back, its undercarriage removed and filled with a quantity of boiling reddish-brown magma.

I was given bread and some sort of earnest warning, which I blithely ignored, dipping in and scarfing greedily, bubbling all the skin off the roof of my mouth. It was complete agony… but it was also so good that I couldn't stop, shovelling in more and more, blistering the blisters, until every last scrap was gone.

Serving hot, spiced crab in its shell is a lovely bit of table theatre. Devilling it also allows you to use frozen crab quite happily if you're not lucky enough to be able to grab one off a day boat in Lisbon harbour. Some supermarkets now sell 'dressed' crabs in the shell from their fish counters, which are perfect for this job.

Chop a shallot very finely and clarify it in butter in a hot pan. Add a shot of sherry and allow it to bubble off, then slip in a couple of large lumps of *sobrasada*. Throw in a large handful of breadcrumbs, the contents of your dressed crab and a large spoonful of crème fraîche. Take the mixture off the heat, stir quickly to combine everything, then taste and season. Now spoon the mixture back into the crab shell and top it with a mixture of breadcrumbs, lemon zest and a little grated mild sheep's cheese, perhaps a Manchego or similar – not enough to taste distinctly cheesy, but just enough to bind the crust and boost the umami. Dot the top with butter and then put the shell onto a tray and into a very hot oven, favouring heat from above, if your oven gives you that option.

When the shell comes out it should be handled with extreme care. The top will be browned and bubbling in a threatening manner. You can serve it just as it is, with chunks of sourdough to dip in, or you could spoon it carefully onto toast or make a plain bread sauce slice (see page 198) and serve the crab ladled over it in a concupiscent manner.

Hot, Honeyed Pig-dip

The simplest dip I know is also the most glorious. It works best with
Spanish or Italian bread – bland, unsalted and just screaming out for
something salty/spicy/fermented/sweet. Take a big lump of *'nduja* or
sobrasada (they are remarkably similar, being cured pork with garlic and
hot pepper, stingingly hot and funky with ferment) and place it in a small
ovenproof dish. A *cazuela* would be appropriate. Heat it in the oven until
the meat becomes soft, the fats become liquid and maybe there's a slight
hint of crisping and browning on the surface.

Drizzle honey over the top. Strong stuff, not that weak nonsense that
comes in a squeezy bottle shaped like a bear, but something heady and
fragrant that tastes like it was made by angry bees. Rip lumps off your
bread and dip it in. You will almost certainly burn your lips. Indeed, you'll
probably go into shock from the chilli hit and endorphins will well up in
your tear ducts… but years later you will still be trying to find my phone
number to call and thank me.

Cook's Perks

Let me tell you a story. A tale of bread dipping, of 'Kitchen Bread' and how it changed my life forever. I was a skinny teenager growing up in a seaside town. I looked, as my games teacher once opined in those crueller times, like 'a twitching, neurotic streak of piss'. When the time came to get a summer job, I lacked the self-confidence or the physical coordination to get past a trial shift as a waiter in a beach café, so I went for a kitchen job at Forte's.

Forte's was an institution in my town. The legendary British–Italian restaurant dynasty had a branch there and owned several monumental dining palaces. The one I was hired into was on the town square – a building containing a traditional tearoom with palms and napery, a more 'modern' cafeteria and an impossibly glamorous carvery and grill room. I believe this occupied the top floor – I know the waiters wore uniforms, anyway, because I remember them yelling at me – and I imagined the room was filled with local Rotarians and their wives quaffing claret. I never ate there… in fact, I never entered the room, because my entire contact with it was at the doors of the lift in the basement wash-up.

Forte's had class – or, at the very least, a brilliant understanding of what the British holidaymaker thought was classy. Though it was serving an unconscionable quantity of egg and chips to people who ate out once a year, there were proper facilities, there were trained and respectful staff and there was a proper kitchen with a full brigade. There were senior chefs in tall hats, distant and imperious. Lower ranks were villainous creatures, often having gained their working experience doing National Service in the Army Catering Corps. Today, when every chef's CV must feature a mandatory 'stage' cleaning mushrooms at Noma, it's difficult to imagine that their forebears 'staged' in British Malaya, making egg and chips as bullets whistled past. They were some of the most worn-out, depleted and vicious human beings I'd ever met and they scared the hell out of me.

Beneath them all, figuratively and literally, in a sub-basement, was me. All the washer-uppers were Italians. Older, rural guys, built low to the ground, covered in muscles and speaking absolutely no English. Their impression when the restaurant manager thrust me into the room, looking like Oscar Wilde's weaker younger brother, in a nylon tunic and a paper hat, was mercifully obscured by the impenetrable barrier of language. I'm betting it wasn't good.

The work was viscerally disgusting. The facilities and equipment were fine, the room ventilated and well-lit and the staff well-trained and efficient. But to a fifteen-year-old whose only experience so far had been helping mum with the dishes – once – it was beyond comprehension. Trolleys came in with swaying piles of plates and cups. Everything from cigarette butts to baby vomit had to be scraped off into a bin. A machine with a long tongue of a conveyor belt had to be fed, constantly. The noise was terrifying and every ten minutes a glass would explode.

We worked for hours and then, quite suddenly, there was a change of pace. The trolleys slowed and the other dish washers moved, unbidden, to other tasks. One began breaking up a delivery of long, crusty 'French stick' loaves. Another poured gallons of orange juice into the big chiller tank. One small man who looked like he knew a thing or two about working with livestock back home slammed cardboard cubes into The Cow (The Cow was a refrigerated cabinet with a tap on the front and each cube contained a plastic sack filled with five gallons of milk).

Then a buzzer sounded, and everyone drifted towards the lift door. The guy who'd been attending to The Cow passed me a loaf and the shift leader handed me one of the huge metal cups that went under the milkshake makers. The doors opened to reveal a wooden trolley and the smashed remains of what looked like half a roast ox.

God knows it was probably just a reasonable-sized roast, but it was big enough to have left ribs standing, with big gobbets of meat still adhering. There was blood-rare meat for those who wanted it, black cracklings for those who preferred them and under everything a thick pool of jellifying juice and fat.

I want to say we fell on it in like animals – the ancient buried drives of Italian peasants, surfacing from lymbic depths of satyric orgy. Actually, it was one of the most weirdly polite meals I've ever eaten. Six disgustingly filthy, sweaty men, offering each other food, pointing out choice pieces, introducing me to the etiquette as surely as Bedouin horsemen at a feast.

We drank milk and orange juice by the litre, built absurd sandwiches and dipped them in the mess on the silver plate. We laughed as the juices ran down our chins. Someone belched. The leader considered the noise, then nodded, as if it was his to mark out of ten and he was minded to be generous.

The bread, by today's standards, was barbarous. It was fluffy, soft and white in a way I now know could only be achieved with machines and additives. The crust was elastic, sweet and a sort of caramel brown that bespoke all manner of interventions in its making. It had no redeeming features. But plunged into these juices… not just dipped into a modest superfluity of gravy or crumbled into a polite soup, but dug deep into an absurd excess… so much juice that we'd probably have to throw some of it away… running down our arms, spilling onto the floor… juices concentrated by heat, insanely over-seasoned. The plenty was intoxicating. You could feel the stuff radiating through your body like a shiver.

I grew, that summer. I grew a lot. I remember the diet that I'd eaten at home, that most of my friends would have recognised, was austere. Roast meat was for Sunday. Dipping bread was impolite. 'French' bread was posh. Milk was too expensive to drink by itself and orange juice was offered in shot glasses as a starter.

Every day, under the guidance of the satyrs, I ate and drank a month's worth of the most luxurious ingredients any of our minds could have stretched to. The bread dipped in the juice was more than merely good – the act of dipping it was a rebellion against the restrictions of my childhood, a thrilling little political gesture against the small-town plutocrats upstairs. It bonded me to the dish washers, to Italians. It showed me that food is more than just itself, the sum of how and where it's eaten and with whom it's eaten. I'm still not sure of the medical truth of it, but I believe I came into the autumn about six inches taller, with huge shoulders, muscles everywhere, grinning like an idiot and looking like a recently sated Viking. My confidence had grown to a ridiculous degree, not from the ennobling effects of manual labour, but from the discovery of my defining vice. I had learned that I loved food and eating more than anything else. I knew who and what I was, and I rather liked it.

I'll probably never get another crack at a carvery cart and a cow carcass, but to this day I revere Kitchen Bread beyond every other dish. Kitchen Bread isn't a recipe – it isn't even a type of bread. It's the stuff you dip in while you're cooking. It's a private vice, just for cooks. It's the 'feedback' loop that tells us that we're doing it right; the way we check ourselves before we deliver to those we love. If your mind works that way (mine doesn't), it's a mildly transgressive thing to do. Dad had a different name for Kitchen Bread – he called it 'cook's perks', and to some degree it is; a little perquisite with which we reward ourselves just before we serve. We have done well… we deserve it. But to me, it's more. It reminds me who and what I am, and I *still* rather like it.

The Team

Making an illustrated food book is about a lot more than just writing it. It's as much of a team effort as recording an album or making a film. I'm lucky enough to be able to work in a particular way with the very best. We're in constant conversation from before pen hits paper and, when we finally assemble for the shoots, we spend weeks together, talking about food, cooking, shooting and eating it. To be honest, these are some of the happiest days in the whole process. Ideas flow, the text changes in response to the pictures, the design develops and all the time the final book is getting better and better. My name might be on the cover, but without these people there would be no book to put it on…

'Snazzy' Harry Webster is the Editor. This means she runs the project, coordinating everything from wrangling ketchup drips on the shoot to hammering my writing into coherence with such cheerful competence that you don't quite notice how steely determined she is. Before she got her hands on it, what you are reading was an incoherent mess. Harry has strong opinions about many foods and seemingly an appetite for all of them.

Sam Folan is the Photographer, who should really have run away when we offered him this gig. We told him it was going to involve dishes that some people might find unappetising, strange, neglected recipes and a lot of brown food. Instead of fleeing, he got a strange look of enthusiasm in his eyes and started turning piles of wet mince into the kind of thing you want to hang on your walls. If you ever need it, and I hope you don't, I reckon Sam could make a dead rat look delicious.

Sarah Lavelle is the Publisher. She's able to look at a very odd pitch, see something in it that I wouldn't have, then guide every step with a light hand until it arrives back from the printers… looking exactly as she'd planned all along.

Luke Bird is the Designer and Art Director. Because he's there, at the early meetings about the shape of the book, and at the table for every single shot, he ties together the look of the whole thing. From the colour of a prop or the prominence of a drip of cheese right the way through to the placement of the last full stop, he makes sure everything reflects the main idea.

Out-of-frame is **Faye Wears**, the Props Stylist, whose diligence and creativity gave life to some very challenging dishes.

Brilliant and talented individuals, every one of them and, as a team – when fuelled by corned beef sandwiches and fine wines – utterly unsurpassed.

I thank them all.

INDEX

A

B

C

M

N

O

P

Q

R

S

Publishing Director Sarah Lavelle
Editor Harriet Webster
Copy Editor Lucy Kingett
Art Director and Designer Luke Bird
Photographer Sam Folan
Props Stylist Faye Wears
Head of Production Stephen Lang
Production Controller Nikolaus Ginelli

Published in 2020 by Quadrille,
an imprint of Hardie Grant Publishing

Quadrille
52–54 Southwark Street
London SE1 1UN
quadrille.com

Cataloguing in Publication Data: a catalogue record for this book is
available from the British Library.

The publisher has made every effort to trace the copyright holders. We
apologize in advance for any unintentional omissions and would be pleased
to insert the appropriate acknowledgement in any subsequent edition.

ISBN 978 1 78713 477 5

Printed in China

Tim Hayward is an award-winning writer and broadcaster. He is restaurant reviewer for the *Financial Times*, a presenter on BBC Radio 4's *The Food Programme* and regular panellist on *The Kitchen Cabinet*. He won the Guild of Food Writers Food Journalist of the Year 2014 and 2015, and Restaurant Reviewer 2017 and 2019, and was the Fortnum and Mason Food Writer of the Year for 2014. Tim is co-owner of Fitzbillies bakery in Cambridge. He is the author of *Food DIY* (2013), *The DIY Cook* (2015), *Knife* (2016), *The Modern Kitchen* (2017) and co-author of *Fitzbillies: Stories & Recipes From a 100-Year-Old Cambridge Bakery* (2019).

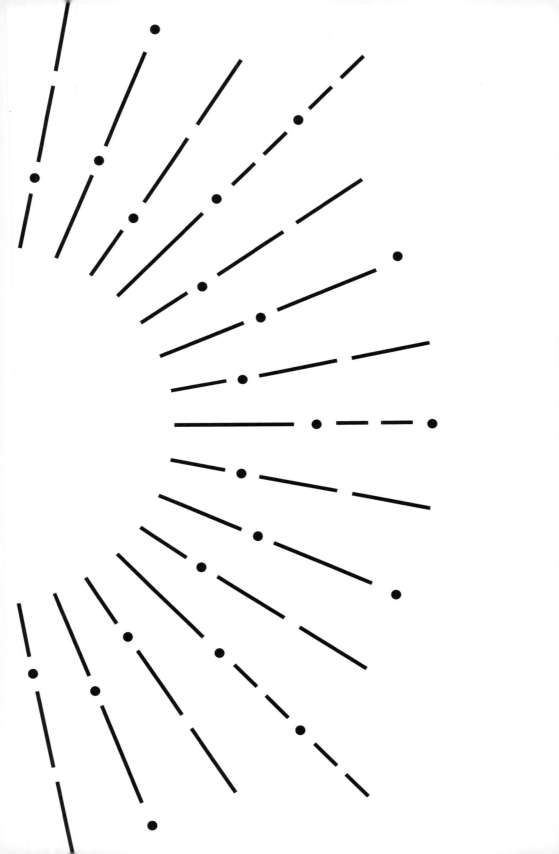

THE RECIPES

Recipe Notes

When writing recipes, there are certain phrases that crop up so often and in such an automatic fashion that they must be as incredibly annoying to read as they are to write. It seems daft to repeat constantly 'good olive oil'. I'm sure your oil is excellent; please don't go out and buy better oil, and anyway, when was the last time somebody wrote 'add two tablespoons of really bloody awful olive oil'. So, unless otherwise specified…

All olive oil is 'good'.

All herbs are fresh.

All eggs are large (US extra-large). (We can hope for free-range, but that is your own decision.)

All butter is unsalted, unless otherwise stated.

'Season' means season to taste with freshly ground black pepper and proper flaky salt.

I also can't, in all conscience, ask you to 'put aside' or 'reserve' an ingredient. It's obvious. Similarly, '…and serve' has been ruthlessly expunged from the last line of every recipe.

DEVILLED KIDNEYS

4 lambs' kidneys
150g (5oz) plain (all-purpose) flour
20g (¾oz) mustard powder
pinch cayenne pepper
10g (¼oz) clarified butter
2 thick slices white bloomer bread, toasted
100ml (3½fl oz) sherry (Amontillado or
*   even 'cream' sherry)*
100ml (3½fl oz) chicken stock (broth)
1 tbsp Worcestershire sauce

Halve the kidneys and remove the cores with sharp scissors (see page 36). Season the flour with the mustard powder and cayenne pepper, and toss the kidney halves in the mixture.

Heat the butter in a frying pan (skillet) over a medium heat until foaming and toss in the floured kidneys. Keep them moving until they are crisp and browned on the surface, about 2 minutes. They should still be pink inside.

Lift the kidneys onto the toast, then pour the sherry into the pan and allow most of the liquid to boil off. Add the stock and Worcestershire sauce, boiling hard and continually stirring so that everything combines to form a thick, spiced gravy. Taste and adjust the seasoning before pouring the gravy over the kidneys. [*See photograph on page 33.*]

SHELLFISH ON TOAST

50ml (2fl oz) olive oil
2 shallots, finely chopped
1 clove garlic, crushed
500g (1lb 2oz) clams or mussels (fresh or frozen;
*   if frozen, cooked as per package instructions)*
75ml (2½fl oz) dry vermouth (if using fresh shellfish)
1 slice sourdough bread
small handful flat-leaf parsley or chervil, finely chopped
salt and black pepper

Warm a little of the oil in a large pan for which you have a lid, add the shallots and garlic and soften. Pour in the cooked shellfish and their liquid, or the fresh shellfish and vermouth. Cover and steam until the shellfish open, about 5 minutes.

Pick the meat from the shellfish shells, discarding any that are unopened. Grill the sourdough on both sides.

Strain the cooking juices back into the pan, bring to a hard boil and add the remaining oil (you could also use cream – 'whipping' is the best). Return the shellfish meat to the pan to reheat in the juices. Season, and stir in most of the chopped parsley. Pour over the grilled bread and sprinkle with the remaining parsley. [*See photograph on page 38.*]

HERRING ROES ON TOAST

500g (1lb 2oz) herring or cod roes (or milt)
2 slices sourdough bread
5g (⅛oz) mustard powder
5g (⅛oz) cayenne pepper
5g (⅛oz) smoked paprika
150g (5oz) plain (all-purpose) flour
150g (5oz) clarified butter
salt and black pepper

Fill a wide pan with salted water and bring to a gentle simmer, then turn the temperature down to low. Drop in the roes (or milt) one at a time and be ready to whip them out with a slotted spoon the second they begin to tighten up – this can take as little as 30 seconds. Line them up on kitchen paper to drain while you toast the bread.

Combine the seasonings with the flour, then roll each roe in the flour to achieve a good coating. Heat half the clarified butter in a frying pan (skillet) over medium–high heat until it foams, then add the roes and roll in the butter until they begin to brown and crisp. Now throw in the rest of the butter and let it melt.

Place the roes on the toast, then spoon over the melted butter and any pan scrapings. [*See photograph on page 45.*]

BACON FAT-FRIED BREAD
WITH MASH AND KETCHUP

300g (11oz) leftover mashed potato
50g (1¾oz) bacon fat
2 slices packaged white sliced bread
tomato ketchup, to serve

Warm up the mash in a pan or a microwave.

Heat the bacon fat in a frying pan (skillet) over a medium heat and fry
the bread on both sides until crisp and brown. Add any remaining fat to
the mash.

Cut each slice of fried bread into quarters, arrange on a plate and top
with a dollop of warm mash. Use the back of a teaspoon to create a 'well'
in the middle of each mash pile and fill it with an immoderate squeeze
of ketchup. [*See photograph on page 51.*]

ONE-EYED EGYPTIANS

2 slices packaged white sliced bread
20g (¾oz) butter or bacon fat
2 eggs
salt and black pepper

Cut a hole out of the centre of each slice of bread with a small wine glass or
biscuit cutter, saving the piece you've cut out.

Heat most of the butter in a frying pan (skillet) over a medium heat and
add the bread and cut-out circles (the 'lids'). Fry for a few minutes until
browned on one side, then flip both, add a dot more butter into the holes
and crack the eggs into the holes. After a few seconds, lower the heat,
season the top of the eggs, then cover the pan. Check often to ensure the
bottom is browned and the eggs are cooked to your liking.

Remove the lid from the pan towards the end so that the bread stays crisp.
Slice the crisp fried discs in half and apply to the well-seasoned eggs 'like
little ears'. [*See photograph on page 52.*]

MINCE ON TOAST

4 slices white bloomer bread, about 2cm
(¾in) thick
800g (1¾lb) beef mince (ground beef)
75ml (2½fl oz) Madeira
1 tsp plain (all-purpose) flour (optional)
1 litre (35fl oz) chicken stock (broth)
2 tsp pickled walnut vinegar (from the jar)
150g (5oz) beef dripping or butter
salt and black pepper

In a dry pan, lightly grill the bread on both sides.

Heat a separate pan over a medium heat and add the mince, along with a cup or so of water. Bring to the boil so that the water 'sets' the mince into distinct grains. Pour in the Madeira and allow the alcohol to boil off. Thicken the gravy with the flour if you wish, but I don't usually bother. Add the stock and simmer for at least half an hour until you're left with mince suspended in a good quantity of gravy. Stir in the pickled walnut vinegar, then adjust the seasoning.

Melt the dripping in a frying pan (skillet) over a medium heat and fry both sides of the grilled bread in it. Transfer to a plate and pour over the mince, allowing the gravy to soak into the bread. [*See photograph on page 55.*]

THE CHIP BUTTY

4 large Maris Piper (or Russet) potatoes
4 slices white 'tin loaf' bread
vegetable oil or beef dripping, for deep-frying
salted butter, for the bread
brown sauce, vinegar or your favourite
chip condiment, to serve
salt

Peel the potatoes and slice them into regular and even chips (fries). Lay the chips on a baking tray lined with a tea towel. Refrigerate, uncovered, for a couple of hours to dry out.

Heat the oil in a large pan to 165°C/330°F and fry the chips in small batches. As soon as the cut surface of the chip begins to bubble but before it takes on any colour, remove the chips from the oil, drain and allow to cool.

Once cooled, butter the bread thickly while bringing the oil up to 185°C/365°F. Fry the chips once more, in small batches. Once the chips have achieved a pleasant brownness, lift them out of the oil, shake to remove excess oil and then lay them onto two slices of the buttered bread and add the lids. Wait a few seconds until the butter begins to melt and soak into the bread, then lift each lid, season with salt and, if you feel you must, add your favourite condiment. [*See photograph on page 72.*]

GRILLED CHEESE

200g (7oz) mixed cheeses (I use Cheddar,
*   Gruyère and a little Parmesan), grated*
butter, for the bread
2 slices white 'tin loaf' bread
mayonnaise (Japanese Kewpie mayonnaise
*   is best), for frying*
salt and black pepper

Make up your custom mixture of grated cheeses and season. Butter one side of each slice of bread. Spread the grated cheese onto the buttered side of one slice and top with the other, butter side down. Press down well. Smear the outside of the sandwich comprehensively with mayonnaise.

Fry the sandwich gently in a dry pan over a medium–high heat, flipping regularly, until crisp and golden. Take things slowly enough that the cheese has a chance to melt before the outside gets too brown. [*See photograph on page 83.*]

'CARPETBAGGER' MONTE CRISTO

1 double-thickness slice white 'tin loaf' bread
20g (¾oz) butter, softened
2 slices smoked ham

2 slices Gruyère
2 eggs
20ml (¾fl oz) whole milk or cream
clarified butter, for frying
salt and black pepper

Cut the crusts off the slice of bread and cut a neat pocket through one side. Butter inside the pocket and insert the ham and cheese. Squeeze closed so that the butter glues everything together.

Beat together the eggs and milk and season liberally, then lay the sandwich in the mixture. Let the sandwich absorb all the egg wash, flipping it regularly to ensure even soaking – including the sides.

Melt the clarified butter in a frying pan (skillet) over a medium–low heat and gently fry the sandwich until crisp, letting it set and heat through without the surface burning. [*See photograph on page 84.*]

PATTY MELT

2 large white onions, sliced
400g (14oz) good-quality coarse beef
*   mince (ground beef)*
4 slices light rye bread
4 slices plastic-wrapped American burger cheese
olive oil, for frying
mayonnaise, for frying
salt and black pepper

Warm a drop of oil in a pan over a very low heat and add the onions. Cover with a lid and sweat gently. They will eventually caramelise to a lovely deep brown, but anyone who tells you this will take less than an hour is lying.

Season the mince well, separate it into two balls and then squish each one out between layers of cling film, baking paper or foil. Use a rolling pin or your hands, but aim for roughly the same shape and size as your slices of bread. Heat a frying pan (skillet) and dry-fry the patties so that the outside browns but the centre remains rare, about a minute each side.

Assemble the patties and bread into two sandwiches, topped with the burger cheese and caramelised onions, and slather the outside of the sandwiches with mayonnaise. Heat a frying pan or sandwich toaster and toast until the cheese is melted and the bread browned and crisp. [*See photograph on page 89.*]

ULTIMATE TUNA SALAD

500g (1lb 2oz) tinned tuna chunks in oil
mayonnaise (Japanese Kewpie mayonnaise is best), to taste
2 sticks celery, very finely chopped
3 spring onions (scallions), finely chopped
30g (1oz) nonpareil capers
salt and black pepper

Drain off half the oil from the tuna, then scrape into a large bowl. Beat the tuna with a large silicone spoonula – the meat will break up and begin to combine with the delicious fishy oil. Season aggressively. Now start adding mayonnaise and continue to beat. You're aiming for a smooth texture, without identifiable lumps of tuna flesh.

Add the celery, spring onions and capers and fold through the mixture. Taste and adjust the seasoning – you will almost certainly need more salt than you're completely comfortable with. [*See photograph on page 97.*]

TUNA MELT

4 slices packaged brown sliced bread
1 quantity Tuna Salad (see above)
4 slices pre-sliced Swiss cheese
gherkins (pickles), to serve

Lightly toast the bread, then dollop with the tuna salad. Top each mound with two slices of cheese, then slide under a medium grill (broiler). The idea is to gently melt the cheese, not bubble and brown it. Once the cheese has properly melted, remove from the grill, top with the remaining slices of toasted bread and squeeze down so that the tuna and cheese squish into a regular layer. [*See photograph on page 98.*]

EGG MAYONNAISE

2 eggs
150g (5oz) mayonnaise
1 tsp Dijon mustard
3 chives, finely chopped
pinch paprika
lemon juice or tarragon vinegar, to taste (optional)
salt (optional) and black pepper

Place the eggs in a pan of cold water, bring to the boil, then turn the heat off and allow the eggs to stand for 10 minutes. Put the saucepan under the tap and run cold water into it. Keep going until the eggs are cold.

Peel the eggs and break them up loosely with a fork or your hands. There should be just the tiniest hint of runny right at the centre of the yolk. Add the mayonnaise, mustard, chives and paprika, and season with black pepper. Stir through gently. Taste and add lemon juice or tarragon vinegar, if you like. These will add acidity, which is entirely a matter of taste – as is the salt.

TAMAGO SANDO

1 egg
4 slices soft white sliced bread
butter, for the bread
1 quantity Egg Mayonnaise (see above)

Steam the egg for 7 minutes, then drop it immediately into iced water. This unusual process should give you an egg that still has a touch of golden softness in the centre but with a fully set white.

Slice the crusts off the bread and lightly butter. Dip a very sharp knife in water and slice your cold, peeled egg lengthways. Place the cut eggs in the middle of two slices of the bread, then mound up the egg mayonnaise around them. Put the top slice onto the *sandos* and press gently to distribute the egg mayo without crushing the central egg half. Slice across with a devilishly sharp knife to reveal the perfect cross section of egg.
[*See photograph on page 105.*]

GRIBICHE-Y TARTARE SAUCE

4 eggs, hard-boiled
20g (¾oz) Dijon mustard
½ clove garlic, crushed
50ml (2fl oz) fruity olive oil
250ml (9fl oz) neutral vegetable oil
2 tsp white wine vinegar (you can use the vinegar
  from the cornichons)
4 sprigs tarragon, leaves picked and chopped
1 bunch chervil, chopped
75g (2¾oz) cornichons, roughly chopped
50g (1¾oz) salted nonpareil capers, rinsed and drained
salt and black pepper

Separate the egg yolks from the whites and, in a large bowl, crush them
to a smooth paste with the mustard and garlic. Drizzle in the olive oil,
whisking continually until it starts to emulsify. Continue adding the
neutral vegetable oil in a steady stream, whisking all the time, for as long as
you can or your nerve will hold, until you have a smooth mayonnaise.

Roughly break up the egg whites with a fork and fold them into the
mayonnaise, followed by the rest of the ingredients. Season. Cover and
refrigerate for a couple of hours, to let the flavours mellow and combine.
[*See photograph on page 115.*]

THE KATSU DOORSTEP

2 pork chops or steaks
plain (all-purpose) flour, for dredging
1 egg, beaten
panko breadcrumbs, to coat the pork
4 slices white 'tin loaf' bread
handful finely shredded white cabbage
butter, for shallow frying
Kewpie mayonnaise or salad cream, to taste
Bull-Dog tonkatsu sauce (or 'brown' sauce), to taste
salt and black pepper

If using pork chops, remove the meat from the bone. Season the meat well, then place between two sheets of baking paper and use a rolling pin to beat it to about 8mm (⅓in) thick.

Dredge the meat in the flour, dip into the beaten egg and then roll in panko breadcrumbs to coat. Be careful to achieve a good coating, pushing down on the cutlet in the crumbs.

Heat a little butter in a frying pan (skillet) over a medium heat and fry the pork cutlets until golden brown and cooked through. (Time will obviously depend on the thickness of your cutlet but a probe thermometer will read 70°C/158°F when properly cooked.)

Top two of the slices of bread with a layer of shredded cabbage, then slice the cutlets into strips and lay over the top. Zigzag the Kewpie over the top in one direction, then turn the *sando* 90 degrees and do the same with the Bull-Dog sauce. Finish with the final bread slices, cut the sandwich in half and Instagram immediately. [*See photograph on page 118.*]

BREAD PAKORA

200g (7oz) gram (chickpea) flour
pinch turmeric, for colour
1 tsp baking powder
1 white onion, chopped
1 tsp pav bhaji masala
300g (11oz) boiled potatoes, roughly chopped
3 tomatoes, roughly chopped
100g (3½oz) frozen peas
6 slices packaged white sliced bread
neutral vegetable oil, for frying
salt

Mix together the gram flour, turmeric and baking powder in a bowl. Season with salt and add enough water to create a coating batter.

Heat a little of the oil in a frying pan (skillet) over a medium heat and fry the chopped onion until softened and golden, then add the *pav bhaji* masala and boiled potatoes to the pan, crushing the potatoes so that they break up. Add the tomatoes and stir through and finally add the peas. Taste and adjust the seasoning.

Cut the crusts off the bread, trimming square, and place a teaspoonful of the vegetable mixture in the centre of each slice. Paint a little of the prepared batter around the edge of each slice and then fold in half diagonally and squeeze the edges to seal into triangular packages.

Heat the oil in a large pan to 175°C /345°F. Dip each package into the batter, then shallow-fry in the hot oil, flipping so that the sides brown evenly. Drain on kitchen paper. [*See photograph on page 123.*]

KARE PAN

400g (14oz) plain (all-purpose) flour
7g (2¼ tsp) instant yeast
275ml (9¾fl oz) warm whole milk
2 tsp salt
1 white onion, diced
1 tsp Japanese curry powder, or 1 curry
  sauce roux block (see page 127)
1 large carrot, diced
2 large potatoes, peeled and diced.
splash soy sauce
1 egg, beaten
neutral vegetable oil, for frying

Mix together the flour, yeast, milk and salt in a mixer with a dough hook. Knead until the dough is smooth and elastic, then divide into eight balls. Place the balls on a floured baking sheet, lightly cover and allow to rise until doubled in size.

Heat a little of the vegetable oil in a pan over a medium heat, add the onion and soften for a few minutes, then add the curry powder (if using), carrot and potatoes. Add a little water to help the vegetables steam through – but not too much – and a splash of soy sauce to season. If using a roux block, dissolve it in a little boiling water and cook the vegetables slowly in it, finishing with quite a dry filling. Leave to cool.

Preheat the oven to 190°C/375°F/Gas Mark 5. Roll out each ball of dough into a 10cm (4in) flat disc, place a dollop of the curry mixture in the middle, then close the dough around it, pinching it closed and rolling into a neat ball. Place back on the baking sheet, leave to prove once more for about 45 minutes until the buns have noticeably increased in size, then brush with the beaten egg and bake until golden brown. [*See photograph on page 126.*]

PRAWN TOAST

1 'thumb' fresh ginger
1 clove garlic
300g (11oz) defrosted, cooked, peeled
    prawns (shrimp)
3 spring onions (scallions), or Chinese chives,
    if you can find them, chopped
1 egg white, beaten
1 tsp soy sauce
½ tsp sesame oil
1 tsp cornflour (cornstarch)
2 slices packaged white sliced bread
15g (½oz) white sesame seeds
15g (½oz) black sesame seeds
neutral vegetable oil, for shallow-frying

Place the ginger, garlic, prawns, spring onions, egg white, soy sauce, sesame oil and cornflour in a blender, then blitz to a paste.

Cut the bread into triangles, then smooth the prawn paste into a neat mound on top of each piece. Spread the sesame seeds on a saucer and push the prawn toast down onto it to coat. Heat the oil in a deep frying pan (skillet) to 185°C/365°F and shallow-fry, flipping occasionally, until golden on both sides. [*See photograph on page 59.*]

PAN BAGNAT
(SALADE NIÇOISE SANDWICH LOAF)

1 day-old white baguette or boule
1 clove garlic
1 tin good-quality tuna in oil
100g (3½oz) fine green beans, blanched
6 black olives, pitted
1 red onion, thinly sliced
2 eggs, hard-boiled and sliced
3 tomatoes, sliced
15g (½oz) nonpareil capers
8 leaves romaine or gem lettuce
Dijon mustard, to taste
fruity olive oil, for drizzling
splash sherry vinegar

Slice the bread in half horizontally and rub the cut face with the clove of garlic.

Drain the tuna badly – it's good to use some of the oil, but you need to allow for some absorptive power for fresh stuff, too. Lay the tuna on the bread in chunks. Top with the blanched beans, olives, sliced onion, eggs and tomatoes. Sprinkle with the capers and cover with the lettuce leaves. Smear the inside of the lid with a little Dijon mustard and then hose on plenty of really fruity olive oil and a splash of sherry vinegar. Close the sandwich, wrap well in cling film and refrigerate overnight under weights, turning once, if you remember, before bed. Allow to come up to room temperature before serving. [*See photograph on page 130.*]

THE MEATBALL SUB

3 Italian fennel-seed salsicce
100g (3½oz) stale white breadcrumbs
250g (9oz) beef mince (ground beef)
7 cloves garlic
½ tsp fennel seeds
½ tsp garlic powder

75ml (2½fl oz) crème fraîche
1 egg, beaten
3 x 400g (14oz) tins chopped tomatoes
1 long, white soft roll or ciabatta
3 slices provolone
Parmesan, to serve
salt and black pepper

Preheat the oven to 200°C/400°F/Gas Mark 6.

Skin the sausages and break them up into a bowl. Stir in the breadcrumbs and combine thoroughly before adding the beef mince. Grate in three of the cloves of garlic and add the fennel seeds and garlic powder. Stir in the crème fraîche and the egg, then form the mix into smooth, egg-sized balls.

Pour the tomatoes into a baking dish with a lid or a heatproof casserole dish along with the remaining cloves of garlic. Put into the hot oven and cook until the sauce is reduced and the top is scorched. Season and blitz with an immersion blender. Move the dish to the stovetop over a low heat, sink the balls into the sauce and put the lid on. Keep just below a simmer, allowing the meatballs to poach in the juice and the flavours to exchange. Once the balls read 75°C/167°F at the centre when tested with a meat thermometer, they are ready to eat.

Split the bread in half horizontally, break the meatballs in half and place on the base in a single layer. Top with the provolone and place, along with the top, under a hot grill (broiler). Once the cheese has melted, remove from the grill, ladle the hot tomato sauce over the cheese and meatballs and sprinkle liberally with Parmesan. Perch the lid on top and serve with loads of kitchen paper. [*See photograph on page 133.*]

THE FRENCH DIP

1 x 750g (26oz) rolled beef topside (top round roast)
2 tsp dark soy sauce
1 tsp garlic powder
1 tsp mustard powder
1 x 400g (14oz) tin beef consommé

500ml (17½fl oz) chicken or beef stock (broth)
1 'sandwich' or demi-baguette, cut in half
mustard or horseradish sauce, to serve
salt and black pepper

Place the beef in a roasting dish and brush with the soy sauce, then refrigerate, uncovered, for two hours until it dries into a sticky coating.

Preheat the oven as high as it will go. Sprinkle the garlic and mustard powders onto the beef and transfer to the hot oven, turning the temperature down to 180°C/350°F/Gas Mark 4 as soon as the door is closed. The meat should take about an hour for rare, which is how you want it, but it's best to check with a meat thermometer – it should be 50°C/122°F in the centre. Remove from the oven and allow to cool.

While the beef is cooking, combine the consommé with the stock in a pan and simmer until reduced by half. When the beef has cooled, add any juices and pan scrapings to the '*jus*'. Taste and adjust the seasoning.

Slice the beef thinly and heap into the split baguette. Add a smear of mustard or horseradish. Serve cold with a cup of the hot *jus* for dipping. [*See photograph on page 134.*]

WINSTON CHURCHILL'S CHEESY FINGERS

100g (3½oz) Parmesan, finely grated
20g (¾oz) fresh white breadcrumbs
125ml (4½fl oz) single (light) cream
2 thick slices white 'tin loaf' bread
clarified butter, for frying
salt and black pepper

Mix together the Parmesan and breadcrumbs and spread out in a shallow dish. Season the cream and pour into another shallow dish.

Cut the bread into thick fingers to create a square cross section and soak them in the cream. Roll the fingers in the cheesy crumbs.

Heat a little clarified butter in a frying pan (skillet) over a medium–high heat and gently fry the fingers, turning regularly, until golden brown. [*See photograph on page 145.*]

SPECULAAS PAIN PERDU

250g (9oz) speculaas or ginger biscuits (cookies)
pinch ground cardamom
pinch ground cassia or cinnamon
pinch ground black pepper
pinch ground ginger
250g (9oz) cold butter, cubed
2 slices white 'tin loaf' or bloomer
2 eggs
15g (½oz) whipping cream (or milk)
clarified butter, for frying
icing (confectioners') sugar, for dusting
salt

Empty the biscuits into a blender and blitz as finely as you can.

Grind the spices and a large pinch of salt in a pestle and mortar. Add the dry seasonings to the biscuit crumbs and continue to blitz, then gradually add the butter. When everything is combined and forming a smooth paste, check the seasonings before packing into a jar and refrigerating.

Sandwich a generous smearing of the *speculaas* butter between the two slices of soft white bread, then cut off the crusts. Beat the eggs and cream together, then dip in the sandwich. Allow to soak for 5 minutes. Fry very slowly and gently on both sides in clarified butter until the outside is crisp. Dust with icing sugar. [*See photograph on page 149.*]

PANZANELLA

1 red onion, finely sliced
2 tsp sea salt, plus pinch
6 large tomatoes, roughly chopped

1 sweet red (bell) pepper, chopped
1 sweet yellow (bell) pepper, chopped
½ cucumber, chopped
2 cloves garlic, crushed
1 tbsp white wine vinegar
30 capers
6 anchovies in oil, roughly chopped
6 leaves basil, torn
½ stale loaf, unsalted Italian or Spanish bread,
*   torn into rough chunks*
fruity olive oil, to taste
sugar, to taste

Put the onion in a large bowl with the salt. Use your hands (I wear latex gloves) to scrunch the onion and salt together until wilted and yielding liquid. Add the tomatoes to the bowl with a pinch more salt, stir and refrigerate overnight.

The next day, add the peppers and cucumber to the bowl along with the crushed garlic. The salad should now be swimming in liquid, so add the white wine vinegar and start adding olive oil, a little at a time, tasting and adjusting the seasoning of the dressing as you go. Add a little sugar if needed. Throw in the capers, anchovies and basil.

By this time there should be a lot of liquid for your bread to soak up. Take a look at the quantities you have and judge – if you don't think there's enough liquid, you can soak the bread in water for 2 minutes, then wring it out, otherwise just toss it all in, stir and let it stand for 15 minutes. Taste again and correct the seasoning before serving. [*See photograph on page 151.*]

GAZPACHO

1 quantity ingredients for Panzanella (see
*   page 241), minus the capers, anchovies and*
*   basil, and swapping the white wine vinegar*
*   for sherry vinegar*
3 cloves garlic
1 sweet red (bell) pepper, chopped

You can blitz leftover *panzanella* into a perfectly serviceable gazpacho if you wish. Alternatively, take the same ingredients and add them to a blender in the same order. Capers and anchovies might make a good garnish, but leave them out of the blender. Basil is not as appropriate as red pepper, so you'll need more red pepper, as well as extra garlic. Add the olive oil last, trickling it in like a mayonnaise and letting the bread in the mix hold it in suspension. Add water to correct the texture to your taste and adjust the seasoning before serving chilled. [*See photograph on page 154.*]

UPMA

10 cashew nuts
2 slices packaged white sliced bread
½ tsp mustard or cumin seeds (or both)
4 dried curry leaves
pinch ground black pepper
½ 'thumb' fresh ginger, grated
¼ clove garlic, minced
1 white onion, finely chopped
1 tomato, finely chopped
1 green chilli pepper, sliced
½ small bunch coriander (cilantro),
*   leaves roughly chopped*
mustard oil or neutral vegetable oil,
*   for frying*
salt and black pepper

Warm a dry pan over a medium heat and toast the nuts until just browned. Remove the nuts and gently toast the bread in the same pan, then remove and tear into small pieces. Put the pieces of bread back into the pan and continue to toast until you achieve a dry, rusk-like consistency. Set aside.

Turn up the heat and pour in the oil to the depth of around 1mm. Add the dry spices and keep them moving until the mustard seeds start to pop and sizzle. Add the ginger, garlic and onion, and turn the heat back down. Sweat the onion until it softens, then add the tomato and chilli and a splash of water. Cook down to a well-combined sauce consistency, then stir through the bread. Adjust the seasoning, then sprinkle over the coriander. [*See photograph on page 157.*]

AÇORDA

For *açorda marisco*, try making this with mixed fish and shellfish and a quick fish stock made from bones, shells and trimmings.

100ml (3½fl oz) olive oil
250g (9oz) chopped toucinho (smoked bacon)
  or chouriço (chorizo) sausage
3 cloves garlic
1 red chilli pepper, chopped
1 large white onion, chopped
1 large bunch coriander (cilantro), leaves and stems separated
500ml (17½fl oz) chicken stock (broth)
1 white rustic loaf, roughly torn into chunks
2 eggs, beaten
salt and black pepper

Heat the olive oil in a large pan over a medium heat and gently fry the bacon or sausage for a few minutes until browned. Add the garlic, chopped chilli, onion and coriander stems and lower the heat so that everything breaks down. Next add the chicken stock and simmer for a while, then add the bread. Keep the heat low and stir regularly until the bread has completely collapsed, about half an hour. You're looking for a porridge-like consistency, so add more stock if you need it.

Remove the soup from the heat and allow it to stand for a few minutes before quickly stirring in the eggs. Do it fast so that they don't scramble too much. Adjust the seasoning and top with the torn coriander leaves. [*See photograph on page 158.*]

FRENCH ONION SOUP

75g (2½oz) butter
1kg (2¼lb) white onions, finely sliced
15g (½oz) plain (all-purpose) flour
150ml (5fl oz) white wine
1.5 litres (53fl oz) chicken or beef stock (broth)
4 slices sourdough bread
250g (9oz) Comté, grated
salt and black pepper

Melt the butter in a large pan over a low heat and add the onions. Keep the temperature low so that the onions take as long as possible to sweat, go soft and begin to gently colour. Allow 30 minutes' cooking time at the very least.

Stir in the flour and cook for a few minutes until it colours and takes on the biscuity smell of cooking, then pour in the wine and allow the alcohol to boil off. Pour in the stock, bring to a simmer and season, then portion out into ovenproof serving bowls.

Preheat the oven to 200°C/400°F/Gas Mark 6.

Cut the slices of bread to fit the bowls as lids, then grill them in a hot, dry pan. Float the toasted bread on top of the soup. Sprinkle the grated Comté messily over the top and put the bowls into the oven. Cook until the cheese is bubbling and browned. [*See photograph on page 161.*]

VALPELLINENTZE

250g (9oz) pancetta, diced
500g (1lb 2oz) savoy cabbage or cavolo nero,
*   stems and ribs removed but leaves left whole*
10 slices white Italian bread
500ml (17½fl oz) rich beef broth
10 slices prosciutto, finely sliced
250g (9oz) fontina, grated
ground cinnamon, to taste
grated nutmeg, to taste
salt and black pepper

Preheat the oven to 180°C/350°F/Gas Mark 4.

In a frying pan (skillet) over a medium heat, render down the pancetta, then add the cabbage and gently sauté the leaves until wilted.

Toast the bread in the preheated oven until crisp, then lay a couple of slices in the bottom of a large, broad, ovenproof serving bowl that will fit in the oven. Warm the broth and adjust the seasoning. Be generous. Pour a little of the broth over the bread, season sparingly with a pinch of cinnamon and nutmeg, then add a layer of the cabbage and one of prosciutto.

Repeat this process until you run out of ingredients, finishing with a layer of cabbage. Pour in more of the broth until everything is just covered. Let the broth soak in for a few minutes and then top up again with more broth. It's important to make sure that everything is completely saturated. Top with a thick layer of fontina cheese. Transfer to the oven and bake for half an hour or so. [*See photograph on page 166.*]

COFFIN BREAD

1 white 'tin loaf'
150g (5oz) clarified butter, melted

Preheat the oven to 180°C/350°F/Gas Mark 4.

Cut the crusts off the loaf, keeping the corners at 90 degrees. Slice the loaf into two or three large, regular cuboids. Slice a 1cm- (½in-) thick 'top' off of each cuboid and then make four cuts down into the bottom piece, creating a 1cm- (½in-) thick wall. Carefully pluck out the interior, leaving a thick bottom. Brush the box and the lid, inside and out, with the melted clarified butter, place on a baking sheet and transfer to the oven. Bake, flipping the pieces regularly, until crisp and golden.

Allow to cool on a wire rack and reheat gently before loading with a filling of your choice. [*See photograph on page 168.*]

LOBSTER CHOWDER

2 whole cooked lobsters (fresh or frozen, defrosted)
30g (1oz) butter
1 white onion, chopped
1 stick celery, chopped
1 tbsp tomato purée (paste)
75ml (2½fl oz) dry vermouth
150ml (5fl oz) white wine
500ml (17½fl oz) whole milk
1 shop-bought sourdough boule
100g (3½oz) clarified butter

2 medium potatoes, chopped into 1cm (½in) dice
1 leek, white part only, finely chopped
1 shallot, finely chopped
100ml (3½fl oz) double (heavy) cream
sriracha sauce, to taste
salt and white pepper

Preheat the oven to maximum.

Split the lobsters in half over a bowl and extract as much meat as you can, being careful to catch any juices. Roughly chop the meat and set aside. Put the shells and trimmings in a roasting tin, breaking up the big pieces. Roast until the edges scorch.

Melt the butter in a large pan over a medium heat and sweat the onion and celery until translucent. Add the tomato purée and cook out for a minute or two until it loses its acidity. Pour in the lobster shells and any juices and, while the tin is still hot, deglaze it with the vermouth, scraping to dissolve any stuck-on and browned bits. Pour the vermouth and bits into the pan with the white wine and simmer, until the volatile 'alcohol' smell has dissipated. Add the milk and bring to just below boiling.

Slice the top off the bread, tear out the inner crumb and tear the crumb into regular-sized pieces. Heat the clarified butter in a frying pan (skillet) and fry the chunks of bread to make golden-brown croutons. Set aside. In the same pan, fry the potatoes with the leek and shallot until softened.

Strain the milky lobster stock through a sieve into another large pan, pushing down hard to extract all the flavour. Add the potatoes, leeks and shallots to the bisque.

Put the loaf into the hot oven and bake until just browned on the inside.

Once the potatoes have cooked through, about 5–8 minutes, stir in the cream and the lobster meat. Adjust the seasoning with salt, white pepper and sriracha, then pour the chowder into the hollowed-out loaf, topping with the croutons. [*See photograph on page 174.*]

ZUNI-INSPIRED ROAST CHICKEN WITH BREAD SALAD

With grateful thanks to Judy Rodgers.

1 large chicken
100g (3½oz) fat sultanas
splash balsamic vinegar
½ rustic Italian loaf, torn into chunks and left to stale slightly
100ml (3½fl oz) olive oil
100g (3½oz) pine nuts
2 bunches watercress
salt and black pepper

Season the chicken liberally inside and out and refrigerate, uncovered, overnight.

Half an hour before cooking, remove the chicken and let rest at room temperature. Preheat the oven to 180°C/350°F/Gas Mark 4. Place the sultanas in a bowl along with hot water and a splash of vinegar until just covered. Leave to soak.

Loosely stuff the chicken with the chunks of bread, place in a roasting pan and roast in the oven until cooked through (the temperature in the thickest part of the thigh should read 75°C/167°F on a meat thermometer). Once cooked, remove the chicken from the pan and pour off and reserve the cooking juices. Pull out the stuffing and toss it in the bottom of the roasting pan. Add the olive oil, some of the chicken fat, the sultanas and their soaking liquid and the pine nuts, and toss so that the bread soaks up all the goodness. Now roast the bread in a hot oven while the bird rests.

Shove the watercress into the back end of the chicken before bringing to the table, then extract it and toss it with the hot bread and carved chicken. [*See photograph on page 176.*]

ROAST CHICKEN ON PANADE

1 chicken, salted overnight
1 stale rustic white loaf, torn into chunks

6 large white onions, finely sliced
50g (1¾oz) butter
200g (7oz) Gruyère, grated
1 litre (35fl oz) rich chicken or beef stock (broth)
salt and black pepper

Salt the chicken generously, inside and out, and tear the bread into large chunks. Leave the bread out to stale, cover the chicken loosely and refrigerate overnight. Caramelise the onions in the butter following the method on page 231.

When you're ready to cook, preheat the oven to 180°C/350°F/Gas Mark 4.

Pack a layer of the stale bread chunks into a baking dish, top with a thin layer of the caramelised onions and then sprinkle over the Gruyère. Build a second layer of bread on top, seasoning as you go, then pour over the stock until you can see it pooling between the bread chunks. Wait a little to ensure that the bread is soaking up the stock, then top up with a little more. Place the chicken on top. Season the top of the bird and transfer to the preheated oven. Cooking time will depend on the size of your chicken – once you reach an internal temperature of 75°C/167°F at the thigh joint, remove the chicken and pour any juices from the cavity into the bread.

Turn the oven up to maximum and, while the chicken rests, slide the bread base back in, until the top is brown and crisp.

Replace the rested chicken on the bread to bring to the table. Serve the bread with a big spoon, making sure you include some crispy bits, some soft stuff, the sweetened onions and some melted Gruyère with each helping. [*See photograph on page 179.*]

BREAD (AND BUTTER) PUDDING

100g (3½oz) butter, softened, for spreading
15 slices malty sliced brown bread
150ml (5fl oz) whole milk
50g (1¾oz) demerara sugar, plus extra for the top
3 eggs, beaten
50g (1¾oz) butter, melted

100g (3½oz) Cape raisins, soaked in 250ml (9fl oz) hot black tea
ground cinnamon, to taste
ground nutmeg, to taste

Preheat the oven to 190°C/375°F/Gas Mark 5.

Lavishly butter slices of the bread and tear into large pieces. Stick the pieces around the bottom and sides of a regular loaf tin.

Tear up the rest of the bread and soak it in the milk. After 10 minutes, you should be able to beat it like a thick batter – if not, add a little more milk. Stir in the sugar, eggs, the melted butter and the soaked raisins (discard the tea). Season generously with cinnamon and nutmeg. The finished mix should be barely pourable. Scrape it into the bread-and-butter-lined tin and bang it on the work surface to remove any air pockets, then top with a thick crust of more demerara sugar. Bake for 90 minutes before turning the oven up to full to crisp the top. [*See photograph on page 183.*]

BREAD 'POND' PUDDING

50g (1¾oz) butter, softened, for spreading
10 slices white 'tin loaf' bread, crusts removed
splash vodka
1 small Navel, Seville or blood orange
100g (3½oz) demerara sugar
100g (3½oz) cold salted butter, cubed

Thickly butter the bread on both sides, and use some of it to line a small metal pudding basin or heatproof bowl. Make sure any gaps are filled. Line with another layer (saving some bread for the lid), trying to ensure that the joins in the first layer are covered by the slices in the second.

Use a clean cloth soaked in vodka to wash the outside of the orange. Over a baking tray, exfoliate the skin of the orange with a little of the demerara sugar, being careful not to lose any. Drop the whole orange into the bread-lined pudding basin, pack the cubes of butter into the crevices, then pour in the exfoliating rub and the remaining sugar.

Make sure that the filling of the pudding comes up to the rim of the basin (if not, add more butter and sugar), then use the remaining buttered bread slices to create a thick bread lid. Wrap everything tightly with cling film.

Screw up a tea towel and place in the bottom of a large pot with a lid. Place the wrapped pudding on the cloth, then pour in hot water until it comes nearly to the top of the pudding basin. Put the pot over a low heat and allow to just simmer, with the lid on, for 3–4 hours, topping up with water from a boiled kettle if necessary. Once cooked, carefully remove the pudding and leave it to stand until you're nearly ready to serve.

When you're ready to eat, turn on the oven to its highest setting. Unwrap the pudding and cover the top with a piece of foil, buttered on the inside and cinched tight over the top of the bowl. Put the pudding on a baking sheet and put into the oven for 10 minutes. Loosen the pudding with a small palette knife and turn out to serve. [*See photograph on page 184.*]

PASSATELLI

100g (3½oz) stale white breadcrumbs
100g (3½oz) Parmesan, grated
100g (3½oz) pecorino, grated
1 egg, beaten
1 litre (35fl oz) strong, well-flavoured
  chicken broth
salt and black pepper

Combine all the ingredients except the broth and work into a soft dough. Add a little cold water if the mixture is too dry. Wrap the dough in cling film and rest in the fridge for an hour.

Once you're ready to cook the *passatelli*, bring the broth to a bare simmer in a wide pan and check the seasoning.

Feed the *passatelli* dough through a *passatelli* press (or use a potato ricer, a *spätzle* maker or even a large-holed skimming spoon) directly into the simmering broth. The *passatelli* will break up a bit as they hit the liquid, then sink and finally float to the surface when ready. Serve the *passatelli* and broth in bowls. [*See photograph on page 189.*]

CRAB CAKES

250g (9oz) cooked fresh crab or 1 pack
    mixed crabmeat
50g (1¾oz) mayonnaise (Japanese Kewpie
    mayonnaise is best)
100g (3½oz) fresh white breadcrumbs
clarified butter, for frying
salt and black pepper

Strip the meat from the crab or open the packet and separate the brown meat from the white. Try to keep any large chunks intact.

Stir the brown meat into a similar quantity of mayonnaise and then weigh the mixture and add the same amount of breadcrumbs.

Add the white meat and fork it through – no need to combine too thoroughly; keep things light. Season and taste while mixing.

Heat some clarified butter in a frying pan (skillet) over a medium–high heat and add a spoonful of the crab mixture. Fry until it's browned underneath. When it's time to flip the crab cake, squish it lightly into a rough patty shape.

Continue frying the cakes in batches until they are crisp, golden and lacy on the surface. [*See photograph on page 190.*]

CROQUETAS

300ml (10½fl oz) whole milk
300g (11oz) panko breadcrumbs
40g (1½oz) butter
40ml (1½fl oz) double (heavy) cream
100g (3½oz) your chosen flavouring
    (cheese, jamón, chorizo, braised leeks, etc.),
    shredded or chopped
plain (all-purpose) flour, for dredging
2 eggs, beaten

oil, for deep-frying (olive oil for authenticity,
neutral vegetable oil for economy)
salt and black pepper

In a large pan, bring the milk to just below a simmer and then pour in
half the breadcrumbs. Allow to soak for 3 minutes, then, if required,
add another handful of breadcrumbs. Keep going until you reach the
consistency of a thick custard. Blitz with an immersion blender, which
will thicken the sauce further. Beat in the butter to enrich the mixture
and adjust the consistency with cream until it feels like a soft dough.
Taste and season.

Fold in your chosen flavouring element. Refrigerate the mixture until cool,
then take a spoonful at a time and shape into spheres or cylinders before
returning to the fridge to set.

Roll the croquetas in flour, then the beaten egg and finally the remaining
breadcrumbs.

Heat the oil in a large pan until it reaches 175°C/350°F, and deep-fry the
croquetas in batches until golden, about 3 minutes. Drain on kitchen paper
once cooked. [*See photograph on page 195.*]

SKORDALIA

3 cloves garlic
75ml (2½fl oz) whole milk
150g (5oz) blanched almonds, toasted
and crushed
3 slices Italian white bread, blitzed
into breadcrumbs
100g (3½oz) well-flavoured olive oil, to taste
lemon juice, to taste
salt and black pepper

Poach the garlic in the milk until it takes on a distinct flavour. Remove the
garlic, then stir the crushed almonds and breadcrumbs into the pan over a
low heat.

Use an immersion blender to ensure the purée is completely free of lumps, then pour in the olive oil in a thin stream until you reach the texture of a smooth hummus. Add a squeeze of lemon juice, then taste and adjust the seasoning. You should be able to clearly distinguish the bread, almond and olive oil flavours. [*See photograph on page 199.*]

FONDUE

100ml (3½fl oz) white wine
2 tsp lemon juice
1 clove garlic
200g (7oz) Gruyère, grated
200g (7oz) Comté, grated
200g (7oz) Beaufort, grated
2 tsp cornflour (cornstarch)
20ml (¾fl oz) gin (trust me)
2 slightly stale baguettes, to serve
freshly grated nutmeg, to serve
black pepper

Pour the wine and lemon juice into a large heavy-based pan and grate in the garlic. Bring to a gentle simmer. Stir in the grated cheeses a little at a time, stirring gently and allowing each batch to melt before adding the next.

Mix together the cornflour and gin to form a slurry, then pour into the fondue and continue to stir. Season to taste with pepper and nutmeg. Serve hot with chunks of stale baguette for dipping. [*See photograph on page 202.*]

QUESO FUNDIDO

100g (3½oz) Asadero cheese or mozzarella, grated
100g (3½oz) Chihuahua cheese or mild
   Cheddar, grated
100g (3½oz) Manchego or a mixture of
   mature Cheddar and a little Parmesan, grated
8 warm tortillas

Mix together the cheeses and either melt together in a small pan over a medium heat, or melt directly on a hot griddle and scrape up onto a plate or warm tortilla to serve. [*See photograph on page 203.*]

FONDUTA

500g (1lb 2oz) fontina or fontal, rind removed
500ml (17½fl oz) milk
8 egg yolks
150g (5oz) butter
1 loaf Italian white bread, to serve
salt and black pepper

Finely chop or coarsely grate the cheese. Prepare a double boiler by placing a heatproof bowl over a pan of water and, as soon as the water is simmering, add the cheese and milk and heat until the cheese is fully melted and the mixture is smooth.

Beat the egg yolks until smooth and homogenous. Slowly pour the yolks into the *fonduta* in a thin stream, mixing thoroughly with a whisk or silicone spoonula as you go. It is important to do this gently, keeping the heat low, so that the eggs don't scramble. Taste and season. Serve with Italian bread for dipping. [*See photograph on page 203.*]

HOT, SPICED CRAB

10g (¼oz) butter, plus extra for frying
1 shallot, minced
100ml (3½fl oz) dry sherry (fino or manzanilla)
100g (3½oz) sobrasada
100g (3½oz) fresh white breadcrumbs,
    plus extra for the top
1 whole fresh dressed crab
75ml (2½fl oz) crème fraîche
65g (2¼oz) Manchego, finely grated
lemon zest, to taste
sourdough bread or toast, to serve
salt and black pepper

Preheat the oven to maximum.

Heat a little butter in a pan over a medium heat and add the shallot. Fry for a few minutes until translucent, then add the sherry and allow it to bubble off.

Next add the *sobrasada* and allow to it melt and break up. Add the breadcrumbs, the crabmeat and the crème fraîche. Take the mixture off the heat, stirring to combine, then taste and season. Spoon the mixture back into the crab shell and top it with a mixture of breadcrumbs, lemon zest and the Manchego. Dot the top with the butter and then put the shell onto a tray and into the oven (favouring heat from above, if your oven gives you that option) until nicely browned.

Serve with chunks of sourdough for dipping, or spoon onto toast.
[*See photograph on page 207.*]

HOT, HONEYED PIG-DIP

1 thick slice 'nduja or sobrasada
plenty of good-quality honey
sourdough bread, to serve

Preheat the oven to maximum.

Place the *'nduja* or *sobrasada* in a small ovenproof dish and bake it in the oven until the meat becomes soft, the fats become liquid and there is some crisping and browning on the surface.

Drizzle honey over the top and serve with fresh sourdough torn into chunks.
[*See photograph on page 208.*]